THE BEST GUIDE TO NAVIGATE BEREAVEMENT UNTIL RECOVERY

RISING AMIDST GRIEF

A PATH OF HEALING, HOPEN AND RENEWAL
FOR PARENTS AFTER LOSING A CHILD

SHEILA WEST

Published by Publish Master

© Copyright 2023 - All rights reserved.

It is not legal to reproduce, duplicate, or transmit any part of this document in either electronic means or in printed format. Recording of this publication is strictly prohibited, and any storage of this document is not allowed unless with written permission from the publisher, except for the use of brief quotations in a book review.

Under no circumstances will any blame or legal responsibility be held against the publisher or author for any damages, reparation, or monetary loss due to the information contained within this book, either directly or indirectly. You are responsible for your own choices, actions, and results.

Legal Notice:

This book is copyright protected. It is only for personal use. You cannot amend, distribute, sell, use, quote, or paraphrase any part or the content within this book without the consent of the author or publisher.

Disclaimer Notice:

Please note that the information contained within this document is for educational and entertainment purposes only. All efforts have been executed to present accurate, up-to-date, reliable, and complete information. No warranties of any kind are declared or implied. Readers acknowledge that the author is not engaging in the rendering of legal, financial, medical, or professional advice. The content within this book has been derived from various sources. Please consult a licensed professional before attempting any techniques outlined in this book.

By reading this document, the reader agrees that under no circumstances is the author responsible for any losses, direct or indirect, which are incurred as a result of the use of the information contained within this document, including but not limited to errors, omissions, or inaccuracies.

Disclaimer: Names, places, identifying characteristics, and other key details may have been changed to maintain anonymity and protect privacy.

Interior Design by FormattedBooks

DEAREST READERS
GET YOUR FREE GIFT!

BOOK DESCRIPTION

There's a distinct pain to losing any loved one. The pain you will experience when losing your child, your own flesh and blood is the most devastating thing you will ever go through. There is no difference between the age of the child. You will never be experienced in what to expect. There is nothing to provide you with a guideline because few understand that the grief process of parents over the loss of a child takes on a completely different form and the emotions of one spouse may be at opposite ends of the spectrum.

We will investigate some real life situations of individuals who have gone through different scenarios.

- Regardless of the type of death their loss is no less real.

- Styles of grief will never change but the way we work through them is far from linear.

- Is it possible to tie down a list of emotions? Is there a recipe for working through each of them?

- Despite all the raw emotions we are trying to work through, how many other casualties are we leaving in our wake?

- Can you work through your grief, and potentially help those around you along the way?

- How can you find joy, happiness, and peace amidst what was once chaos.

Is there a recipe to working through some of the darkest days of your life as a parent losing a child. There is no difference between step-children or adoptive children, a child in your care has a close enough relationship to rip the heart out of any parent or caregiver.

CONTENTS

Introduction.. xi
Behind the words: Meet the Author..................... xvii

Chapter 1: The Void in my Heart......................1
   Key Takeaways..8

Chapter 2: Riding the Storm: Navigating Uncharted Emotions and Finding Solace..............9
   Key Takeaways.......................................16

Chapter 3: Grief is an Unspoken Loss................17
   Key Takeaways.......................................30

Chapter 4: Sailing Beyond Grief: Rebuilding, Reconnecting, and Honoring Precious Legacies......31
   Key Takeaways.......................................41

Chapter 5: Journey of the Heart: Navigating the Phases of Grief.........................42
   Key Takeaways.......................................55

Chapter 6: Mending Shattered Pieces: Healing Amidst Loss and Turmoil..........................56
   Key Takeaways.......................................70

Chapter 7: Embracing Shared Sorrow: Finding Unity in Grief...72

Chapter 8: Spotting Rainbows: Seeking Rays of Light Amidst Grief...................................83
   Key Takeaways.......................................88

Conclusion..89
References...101

"Accusations cropped up in her thoughts. I should have checked on him before; I should have known something was wrong; I should have taken better care of him!! Beryl nestled her lips close to the tender spot behind Lyle's ear and kissed him. She breathed in the scent of him—powdery and soft, like the promise of spring rain—and keened quietly into the crook of his neck."

Jenny Knipfer (2021)

INTRODUCTION

> "There is a sacredness in tears. They are not the mark of weakness, but of power. They speak more eloquently than ten thousand tongues. They are the messengers of overwhelming grief, of deep contrition, and of unspeakable love."
>
> **Washington Irving (GoodReads, n.d.)**

Your mind swirls. You will never forget those words, or the situation you find yourself in when you lose a child, no matter their age. Whatever the reason, parents will relay the same kind of message. Numbness sets in followed by a wave of nausea. You are disoriented, incoherent, and may even experience anxiety because of an experience you would never wish on anyone.

How can you ever forget that phone call in the middle of the night from where your child had been visiting. That knock on the door—patrolmen drenched in rain, letting you know your child is dead. You feel everything fade, having to find something or someone to yourself just hearing the words. It cannot be! You just spoke with him an hour ago. The patrolmen must be wrong. There is just no way. They are however right as they confirm certain personal items found at the crash site. Everything was his. He had a driver's license and knew how to drive. Torrential rain was falling. Matt had no idea that moving the steering wheel ever so much to avoid a deer in the middle of the road would result in paying the price with his life.

Perhaps you have been given the gift of time with your child. Nobody ever wants to talk about cancer. Too many of these cases result in death. Despite us knowing our time on earth is finite and we each have a time to die, why this? Why so cruel?

If you could choose, this would be one of the least favorite choices. Given there are so many different types of cancer to choose from—Not as though the outcome is ever different. You question yourselves, where to go from here. Still numbed out by shock, disbelief, and an inconsolable amount of pain. You know this makes it all go so much worse than it needs to be. At the time, you don't think clearly; how can you?

You think of all the pain of chemo and radiation. What the side effects of each of these treatments will have on your beautiful, perfect, child. How do you explain to them sufficiently for them to decide for themselves. You know what comes with these treatments. Endless, ongoing tests, poking, and prodding. Constant trips to the hospitals. Due to her age, she may even be placed in a specialized cancer wing just for children. She can interact with peers going through the same thing. Then there's the nausea, and other excruciating side effects that you, as her parents would gladly take on if you could.

Do you choose this option, knowing full well what you are signing up for, or do you go the alternate route. Minimum, less invasive treatment where your daughter remains at home, living life to the full. Allowing her to continue doing the things she loves. Spending precious time with you as parents, friends, and other loved ones.

Sure, you know there will come a day when her health will begin to deteriorate. You have discussed all of this with her before. She knows she is dying but is glad for the time to say goodbye living life on life's terms.

Choosing to do nothing, may result in a slightly shorter lifespan but her quality of life has been so much better. She got to live out some of her dreams, spending quality time with those who desperately loved this little ray of sunshine. Conscious time allowed you to prepare her for what was going to take place. You have been able to be counseled, prepared by Hospice, and possibly even additional religious support.

Despite all your support, as parents, and preparation, the pain remains just as real! For however much time you still have with your daughter, it will never be enough. Your hopes will forever be dashed. You can be grateful for the chance to be able to hold her hand as she peacefully closes her eyes. You squeeze her hand—thinking how tiny it is in yours. You cry, as you feel the life leave her body. One might have the chance to bid farewell, recognizing a life well lived. At least as full as you could make it during the time she had left. This doesn't make your pain any less real than that of those children who were taken immediately. It is possibly, even more painful. They got to live with hope daily. Waking each morning asking whether today was her last.

Each of these examples have two things in common—death, and inconsolable grief.

How do you explain an emotion so raw, personal and individual that even when two people, say parents, go through exactly the same experience, yet the pain can be so completely different?

All those worn-out, cliché, rote attempts at consolation come across as hollow words. It is impossible for anyone to have any concept of what you are feeling or going through. How can anyone try and explain away your absolute devastation? That pain that targets your gut. Occasionally you may open up to those that have perhaps lost a child themselves. The reality is that their experience will never be the same as yours. These emotions are totally fluid.

The worn-out rote attempts at consolation come across as just hollow words. How can anyone say they truly know how you are feeling, or what you are going through? The only people you feel you can communicate with are those who have experienced the loss of a child. There is mutual understanding of those emotions you may be experiencing!

You want to scream each time you hear the words, "I'm so sorry for your loss." The words just won't come out. Eventually it feels like those tears have dried up. You are all cried out. Till just memories fill your mind and suddenly those floodgates begin to flow once more making the entire world hazy. Trickles of salt run down your cheeks. An empty box of tissues has each been transferred crumpled and tear-stained into a wastebasket. Not all of them make it. Who cares? One of your entire purposes for existing has been snatched away from you. You know that life must go on. It simply must. You have others depending on you. What does that matter though when you feel as though your whole world has been ripped out from under you? Part of you died alongside your child that day.

The truth is that grief never goes away. Those who optimistically say that "time heals all wounds," or "life gets easier as you learn to accept it," have possibly never had to experience such a loss that the only thing you know for certain is that your life will never be the same again. Time, indeed, doesn't heal any wounds. Sure, you may learn to cope a little more as one month becomes two, one year turns into a decade. Memories remain, irrespective of how much time passes.

You will always be exposed to certain triggers. You may suddenly be overcome by grief, moving you into a state of anxiety or depression because your memories are too painful to bear. It is times like these when leaning on your support structure is vital. Decades later, the pain is still there. There will always be those moments. Moments in time where recollections of events can be so vivid that you feel you can feel the texture of the fabric they wore. You remember the distinct smell of their perfume, or deodorant. You remember that sweet, perfectly innocent scent that only comes with a newborn. You can suddenly hear them laugh—or at least convince yourself that you do. Birthdays come and go, but you celebrate them anyway. Each of these are etched in your mind never to be erased by time.

You find yourself lost in thought. Smiling at something you know they would have loved. You wish their phone would ring once more. Just to hear their voice, share your burdens, and often just tell them about your day or tell them how much you love them. Sometimes you are plagued by the fact you never expressed your love often enough.

You know this type of behavior is unhealthy. It is a compulsion. A way for you to try and remain connected with who they are, and who they were. You will be forgiven for seeing a child that even vaguely resembles them either becoming a trigger, or an icon. You can sit and watch them as long as possible.

What I have discovered about grief is that trying to work through your emotions, identifying them and learning how to process them as and when they happen can make things more bearable. I'm not saying that it is as simple as changing your mindset or your environment. From my own experience I have worked through so many different coping mechanisms and ways of dealing with grief. I am still working on them. I think there will always be something holding us back from totally processing our loss.

When it comes to what is known as the stages of grief, I think I have skipped my way through all of them. There have been times when I have been angry. Angry with the world, angry at God, angry at society, the medical profession, and probably the most destructive of all—angry with myself. I have been so numbed out by loss that I was stuck in denial for seven years before I could finally face the truth. I wasn't "fine." I wasn't "coping." I wasn't "handling it." And I most certainly hadn't accepted it.

The problem with denial is that there comes a time when you must face your fears. You must come to terms with your experience. Your loss. By denying the truth for an extended period, I had unknowingly avoided processing my loss and confronting my grief. Not effectively. Not at all really. It was no wonder that finally coming to terms with something so life-changing all those years later would lead to so much emotional stress that it resulted in a nervous breakdown.

That's the problem with not working through grief—it will always come back around until you find a coping mechanism that works for you.

Grief can potentially be a liberating and empowering experience. This is certainly not a one-size-fits-all solution to every situation, and I do not promise your pain will immediately disappear. I can share that there is hope. Hope that healing is possible. Hope that you can find the peace you so desperately seek, and hope that your life can continue. The dark clouds will clear, allowing shafts of sunlight to once again provide you with the peace and warmth you deserve, as, and whenever you need it.

BEHIND THE WORDS: MEET THE AUTHOR

Sheila West is an avid reader, an adventurous pioneer and above all is extremely passionate about living life. After the death of her sister, this will and passion inside her seemed to have died as well. She knew she had to do something about the way she was feeling or she would be overcome with emotion and grief continuously.

Sheila researched the effects that death, and the loss of a loved one can have on individuals and on various aspects, whether emotional, physical, mental, or even spiritual. While working with others, she discovered this was much worse when it came to parents or individuals losing a child.

She has dedicated her life to helping others learn to fill that void or at least providing them with some of the coping mechanisms to do so.

CHAPTER 1
THE VOID IN MY HEART

> "It took an instant to lose you, and it will take my entire LIFETIME to grieve the loss of you. GRIEF never ends because LOVE never ends. I will love you and ache for you until my very last breath."
>
> **Angela Miller (Tampa Bay Compassionate Friends, n.d.)**

The love a parent feels for their child can be described as intensely pure love. It combines each joyful emotion. Ones that are mainly happy making you feel content with your life. These emotions empower you as a parent, and help you let your child know how much they are loved. You show them this by expressions of affection. You hug and kiss them, as they get older this might turn into a fist bump or a high five, but each of you know what it means.

It should be mentioned at the beginning of this journey that the bond between a step-child or an adopted child is exactly the same. They would have crept into your hearts just as much as if they were your own flesh and blood. When you made the decision to marry, or bound yourself to another parent with children, you become very much part of their lives. Your hurt can be no less painful than if they were your own. Don't allow anyone to try and take this away from you or treat you differently because of this.

THE INTENSE BOND BETWEEN A PARENT AND A CHILD

To those around they are your pride and joy. You take each opportunity to let others know how wonderful they are. Of course, you leave out all the mischievous stuff they get up to. The stuff where you may have had to punish them or raise your voice above its normal tone to get your point across that you are the adult in the relationship.

It has become harder to remember when you first arrived home from the hospital with this brand new bundle of a minute human being. You were in awe that this was something you and your spouse had created. Everything about them was so perfect. They even smelled brand new. You battle to find words to describe the pure amazement, joy, and overwhelming love you feel. For many they can't contain themselves and feel they might just burst with pride.

At this time all you want to do as parents is protect this tiny soul gifted to your home. You decide to be the best parents in the world, without realizing this would be an impossible task to ever fulfill.

While still little you can spend hours watching them sleep, counting tiny fingers and toes over and over again. You love the way they fall asleep on your chest while you rock them gently. This period of feeling completely in awe of this tiny human being is short-lived. It is way too short.

They begin to grow and you soon discover that growing pains aren't just for kids, parents experience these changes alongside their children. Only this is through the lens of parenthood and how to raise a toddler! There will be bouts of exhaustion chasing after them, cleaning kitchen floors all over again where muddy little footprints had run through the house, totally ignoring the fact you had asked them to avoid the kitchen for a while.

Little handprints appear as a result of a lesson in finger painting at kindergarten. The only difference is them using the walls as their canvas. You get them to help you clean the walls in an effort to teach them accountability or consequences. Only to have them do it again in a week's time, the real lesson having gone straight over their little heads.

You find you can forgive them painting black spots on your labrador after watching Disney's *101 Dalmations*. Besides, Fred the golden labrador didn't seem to mind, and once again this was nothing that couldn't be washed out with a good bathing of the dog! You are grateful that the paint is washable. It seemed like a win all round, except for you having to keep the dog still enough while you tried to shampoo him down.

Soon enough they would turn into that pimply faced tweens or teen who had finally stood up to that bully and returned home with a black eye but a sense of satisfaction. They would wear their black eye like a badge of honor, it would help keep bullies at bay for the future.

You offer as much support as you can but all of these are steep learning experiences for parents. Nobody provided you with a handbook on raising teenagers. You resolve to just do the best you can. Horrified at how much things had changed from when you were a teen. Was this how your parents felt about you? Did you push the boundaries as much as you could? For some reason mentally, your childrens teen years are all a daze and the only thing you and your spouse can agree upon is to work as a united front.

There are days when you may have had to send your son or daughter back to their room to change into something more appropriate for school. All the while you can hear them mumbling about you under their breath. Rather than them getting a reputation from peers that are even more cruel than a nagging parent.

By the time evening came you would be exhausted, just wanting to turn in for the night knowing it would be washed, rinse, and repeat the next day. On your way to bed you would have to shout outside your teenage daughter's door to get off social media and do her homework assignments. One of your son's needed to turn down the volume of whatever type of music he was listening to, the other needed to be scolded about still playing video games which he had been instructed an hour or so before to stop doing.

You remember thinking to yourself that kids nowadays were completely different than you were as a child.

The moment you hear of your child's death all these thoughts, feelings, emotions of joy and happiness are instantly replaced with those that take you to that deepest, darkest abyss of misery and hopelessness.

There's no easy way to describe how devastating this loss can feel. Intense grief wraps itself around you like a boa constrictor, unlikely to let go until all the air is sucked out of you. Your focus moves from your upbeat, positive, self to simply being numb. You feel like you are hollow, a shell of your former self. Although your spouse is going through exactly what you are, or that's what you imagine, you somehow find a way. You find the strength to support one another. Both of you are gutted by the loss.

You fight against accepting it is true. A child should be burying their parents when they are much older and have lived a full life. It is not meant to be the other way around where parents bury their child.

Funeral arrangements are normally made with fairly little input from parents as they try to find the perfect outfit for their child to be buried in… What was that favorite flower, song, poet, individual they aspired to be. This is done without too much thought yet intense thought about what their child would want. Emotions are still raw and feelings of being stunned or zoned out make you feel even more depressed. You are grateful for all the assistance extended family offers and gladly accept.

You don't even get time to mourn at the funeral. There are so many people suddenly wanting to speak to you. It's all too much. The only respite can be found in a bathroom where you can cry and get rid of some of the depressive emotions you are feeling. You can't quite put a name to what they are but you have never felt these emotions before. They are so painful you feel your soul being ripped apart. You cannot comprehend a This pain cannot be explained unless you have been there yourself.

Bouquets and bereavement cards start flooding the home, each a reminder of your child and the void in your heart now they are gone. You can't even bring yourself to read any of the cards. Of course, you will have to in due time, but that time is not now.

You find yourself sitting in their room, or lying on their bed, sobbing! It is your form of comfort or release. You don't feel any of your pain relieved. Perhaps it's clutching their favorite top or jacket, holding it close to your chest, just being able to smell the scent of their favorite deodorant, perfume, or fragrance. All you want to do is be able to hold onto something of theirs for a little longer.

Your brain keeps on trying to trick you into thinking that there must be some mistake. You imagine your child has just gone on an extended vacation and would walk through the door at any moment, exactly the same exasperating teen.

Some parents find comfort in leaving their child's room completely untouched. For others the room may be kept dust free and tidy, awaiting their loved one's return. Many simply refuse to open the door again. Maybe because once they open the door all the wounds of loss will flood them like a dam wall, ready to burst any second. Another choice might include boxing up all their child's belongings, each box carefully and lovingly marked. Although the boxes may take up a 'sacred space' in the attic or garage, there's not that constant reminder walking past their room each day.

Everyone grieves differently but it is all out of love. Reasons for doing this may be their form of a coping mechanism.

If all the hurt, anger, frustration, pain, guilt, remorse, sadness, hopelessness and grief has been tucked away behind that door for who knows how many years, suddenly shows signs of cracks, and becoming overwhelmed looks as though it is happening to anyone in the family, is when a solid support structure needs to be in place. Without one, this will be the single greatest trial, and challenge any parent, and family will have to face and try to overcome.

Even if the grieving process happens immediately, the strongest possible safety net should be there to catch them, hold them, and help them through with whatever they need.

If you could imagine all the hardships and challenges any individual will ever experience during an entire lifetime, the single most painful of these is having to face losing your child. Unless you have experienced this firsthand, you cannot comprehend the kind of pain and agony parents and even other family members are going through.

If you are reading this as a parent having just gone through this or maybe still facing year upon year of pain that never seems to go away, you can understand and offer genuine comfort to those other bereaved parents. That nagging question of 'WHY' can possibly be answered through simply sharing your story, the pain and emotions you felt and are possibly still experiencing with others. You know first hand, what this loss feels like, you get it. Nobody else can sit you down and give you their advice unless they have been there themselves.

Initially, in the early stages of living through this pain, there are moments when it eases up slightly, becoming more bearable. You begin to find ways to cherish and remember the good times—the laughter, the shared moments. These memories gradually infuse your outlook with a touch of positivity, even if it's more fleeting than you've felt in a long while. Over time, your family adapts, discovering new coping strategies to navigate life without the presence of your beloved child or sibling. Your communication evolves, deepening the connections between you all, particularly on those challenging days when the weight of loss feels particularly heavy.

Years may go by and although you can't say you no longer feel pain but there are more good days than bad. Something, somewhere will hit a trigger switch, and there, suddenly, every ounce of pain comes flooding back as if it had just happened. It may be so devastating that for a time you battle to function normally. There is no cure for this, unless you have sought third party medical intervention. Other than this, the only thing is time.

Some parents lean on their faith and come to that place of acceptance slightly sooner than others. Don't for one moment believe that this minimizes their pain. Some parents may have this faith completely shattered. They choose to blame God. Their only communication with Him is to ask one single question… "Why my child?" They question their faith. Why had God let this happen to them? Why not someone else's child. This is especially true when others survive the same predicament. They have always been strong members of the congregation of the faith they belonged to. That single question that is asked time and time again—"Why me?" "Why our family?"

All they see in that exact moment is the injustice of it all. All around them they see unworthy parents still abusing and abandoning their children. They see innocent children having to pay the price for the addictions of two individuals they call parents. They weep for them, knowing they would be much better parents. No matter how they think or feel at that moment, it will have no impact on the reality they have to face.

Naturally, if you look hard enough you will see whatever depravity is out there. Things that had your child still been alive you wouldn't have given a second thought to. You can now recognize that there is no stronger bond than that between parent and child. There has never been. Not even the bond between you and your spouse despite the fact that the child you have just lost is a combined product of each of you. Shared DNA. This may take a long time to realize, often by then it is too late.

KEY TAKEAWAYS

- **Embrace the Unique Bond:** Acknowledge the indescribable connection between a parent and child. It's a personal and profound bond that defies explanation and should not be overshadowed by your grief.

- **Practice Self-Compassion:** Release self-blame and self-pity. Remember, blaming yourself won't change the circumstances, and it's crucial to be gentle with yourself during this painful journey.

- **Take it One Step at a Time:** Approach each day as it comes. Sometimes, focusing on just an hour at a time can help you navigate the overwhelming waves of emotions on this rollercoaster of grief.

- **Respect Diverse Grieving:** Understand that grief is a deeply personal experience. Others in your family may express their pain differently, and that's okay. It doesn't diminish their sorrow.

Your Path to Healing: The journey to healing is uniquely yours. Embrace this process and work towards finding a sense of peace in your own way and at your own pace.

CHAPTER 2

RIDING THE STORM: NAVIGATING UNCHARTED EMOTIONS AND FINDING SOLACE

> *"Grief, I've learned, is really just love. It's all the love you want to give, but cannot. All that unspent love gathers up in the corners of your eyes, the lump in your throat, and in that hollow part of your chest. Grief is just love with no place to go."*
> **Jamie Anderson (Your Tango, 2021)**

With every loss, your mind will constantly be filled with questions. These questions seem to be never ending and can hit you hard. Strong emotions can occur at any time catching you off guard. A lot of these questions surround the death of your child, no matter how old they are. Even those who die at birth, shortly after birth through adolescence, and even older children who are no longer living at home, there will always be questions that you feel you need answers to.

Death comes with its own set of emotions. As parents or caregivers, having never experienced anything like it, there's no way to even begin to prepare yourself for the shock, and feelings of overwhelming loss, feeling detached from the world, confusion, and indescribable grief. Emotions surrounding the loss of your child and emptiness bring emotions that differ from person to person, and even how different a mother and father may feel. Can this be tied to 'nature versus nurture?' Gender of the child? Age of child when they died?

Reasons why parents grieve differently is because each of them are their own individuals. They process things differently regardless of how close-knit they are or how strong their bond.

The sudden loss of a child can cause you to react completely differently.

Your initial emotion may be to rationalize and convince yourself you are dreaming. You will soon wake up and nothing would have changed.

Perhaps you become hysterical or numb just staring into the distance from the shock of the news.

You may feel waves of hollow sadness washing over you. At times these waves make you feel like you are drowning in a sea of emotions dragging you down and you can't see a way forward. You feel like there's this weight on your chest, preventing you from breathing. You are not even sure whether you want to… What is life for if it can be so cruel?

RIDING THE WAVES OF EMOTION

Despite wanting to fight all these emotions or deal with each as they hit you there's no way to stop them from coming. You are out of control. You know it, you don't like it but there is nothing you can do about it.

Perhaps you feel you are having an outer-body experience, watching as everything unfolds where you want to shout out to yourself but the words won't come out.

Just some emotions might be shock, fear, dread, anger, sadness, emptiness, overwhelm, and even peace. You may question how any parent can feel peace when losing a child. This peace comes if you have watched your child fighting a terminal illness each day. Going through extensive painful procedures in an attempt to fight off whatever diagnosis they have received. This death may be one of peace. The peace that there is no longer excruciating pain. No longer waiting for that phone to ring, or traveling from home to the hospital, perhaps being at their bedside for extended periods of time. This diagnosis and suffering involves the entire family. Each member will walk their own path when death eventually comes. Irrespective of what emotions you may be going through at times, relief does come, eventually.

Unfortunately by this time in your life you will possibly have lost a loved one. This could be anyone from a parent, grandparent, great-grandparent, other significant family member or really close friend. You can recall how you felt during this loss. At the time you may have been devastated, felt robbed of years and more special moments with this individual.

Perhaps around the time you recognized they were blessed with an incredible life, rich and full of happy times with those around them who cared for them. If they are grandparents you may have some feelings of regret. You may wish that if you had spent more time with them they may have taught you to cross-stitch, or taken you to their cabin in the woods to spend a weekend fly-fishing. The worst regret of all may be for things left unsaid. Time you could never have back.

No emotion shares common ground with any emotion you may feel losing anyone else. You feel the finality of it all. You know your life will never be the same again and there will be a hole in your heart forever. At the time you don't realize that you will be walking into a landmine when it comes to your relationships. These relationships include the relationship with your spouse or partner. The way you treat and interact with your other children, and even how you act toward other members of your immediate and extended family. It is only when you can recognize for yourself that they are also hurting, they have also been affected by such a tragic loss that you can begin to work on the way you are feeling. Only then can you begin to work on the way you feel toward them. The turning point for these relationships is finding common ground. This could be extremely difficult when you are going through so many emotions within yourself that you can't even begin to cope with working on the emotions of others.

Nothing in this world can prepare you for the emotions you feel as a parent when you lose a child. The intensity of emotions are so painful and mind-numbing that you can perhaps even feel you no longer have anything to live for. You cannot predict how long or painful these overwhelming emotions will last. There's simply no timetable. The list of feelings you can be experiencing is a long one and who's to say which has suddenly hit you. Multiple reactions to your experience can leave you unable to function normally.

This inability to function may only last for a couple of days or it can take months to recover completely. While you aren't functioning normally don't make hasty decisions that could have long-term, overall effects. Some of these may be life changing. Something that can never be undone. A couple of examples include separation, divorce, moving house because there are too many memories there… Firstly, recognize that you aren't thinking rationally. What you are proposing, or looking to alter will not only change their own lives but will certainly cause a ripple effect of hurting so many more. More often than not, the irrational decision-maker feels the full weight of their decision and they may even take this to their grave.

Paranoia can set in with some parents. Senses are heightened and they incorrectly believe that everyone around them is blaming them for the loss of their child. If you feel this way there's a strong possibility that you agree with their thought process. What follows is a series of "what if," and "if only," questions. You've been to this place before and already know there's no answer. You know the process is fruitless, but you go there again anyway. It means having to go full circle till you get back to the point of accepting what's done. You will never find the answers.

You cannot turn back the clock even though you may be trying to bargain with God, for Him to rather take you and spare the life of your child.

You may question your worthiness of being a parent at all, especially when it comes to your other children. Feeling this way will alienate your children from you eventually. It is worth mentioning that they are experiencing very similar emotions as you are, except they don't have the same kind of coping skills and life lessons that you do. Don't you think that 'abandoning' them at possibly their biggest crises could leave them with permanent emotional scars? This is a crucial time as a family. This is where you need to stand together, supporting one another. Helping each individual as they need help. Being there, no matter what.

GUIDING YOUR FAMILY THROUGH GRIEF

Depending on their ages you may have to sit them down and do your best to explain why their sibling won't be coming home ever again. You may have to explain the concept of time if your children are still quite young otherwise they will incorrectly assume their sibling is just away and they are going to come back. Whatever you do, don't lie to them, planting false hope that their sibling is just away and will return. Rather be supportive of them, as they might battle to understand and process the truth. They may just surprise you and accept your explanation, mourn accordingly, and then offer support to other siblings that may be battling. Many of these children discover that healing comes through service to others. It is amazing how our children are way more resilient than we give them credit for.

Decide early that all channels of communication are always open. No matter how you feel emotionally, take the time to listen to others in your family as well. Emotions are unpredictable for anyone at first. Encourage them to share the way they feel. As an adult, check in with your kids on a regular basis to be sure you aren't missing anything. Extreme emotions can escalate to the point where some form of intervention is needed.

Being supportive could mean getting your entire family involved. At times children don't want to talk to their parents. They may see how you are battling with your own pain and don't want to burden you with more. This is where that strong support structure needs to step up and step in. Children may have a close relationship with a grandparent, aunt, or uncle. Ask your family to be aware of this and offer their support without judgment and even possibly offering advice. The goal is for them to be sounding boards, without adding extra pressure on an already delicate situation by making unnecessary comments.

The one that makes me the most mad, and you will find those that rub you up completely. These are examples of the timeless rote messages, meant to make it easier for you. Instead, they get your blood pumping. Some of these are: "Just give it time. It will get better," or "You know they are always around, don't you," "I can imagine what you are going through…" and, "I will always be here for you to lean on." NO! They don't have any idea of what you are going through, time does not make things better, and the likelihood of them being around when you really hit rock bottom are slim to none.

Check in with your partner. How are they really doing? If your relationship is strong, and you can be there for one another to lean on, you can try and work through all the pain, how each of you are suffering with different things at different times. You already know from earlier sections that the grieving process is fluid rather than linear. There's no timetable with a stopwatch telling you when one particular emotion will strike. Perhaps it is a group of emotions that decided to band together and attack you together. If your mind, and coping mechanism isn't strong enough, this can place immense strain on you as an individual, on all relationships, personal, within the workplace, within the community that you belong to, to your extended family, but most of all to your spouse and your children. You may know through a previous experience of having gone through the same emotions at the time of your child's death what this symptom is so you know where you are headed. Don't allow yourself to get wrapped up in the emotion, which is far easier said than done. Lean on your solid support structure for assistance.

Going through a myriad of emotions can be confusing enough for you as an adult. For once, place yourself in the shoes of your other children. They will hardly be able to even identify what these feelings are, let alone know how to cope with them. There is only so much support they can receive from those around them, other family members, friends, members in the community, and in some instances even strangers. This is where you have to step in. Actually, you should be the first to step in. You need to take on the full responsibility of being a parent, not just during the good times.

Your child loves you, respects you, and most of all needs you now more than ever. Be present for them, even when you feel the walls closing in on your own life. Don't do this alone either. Involve your partner in the support process. It needs to be a team effort as a family unit. You need to work through these gut-wrenching emotions that accompany the death of a child working alongside someone who gets what you are going through. Someone who is feeling your pain, or recognizes pain they may still need to face is probably one of the only solutions.

The emotions mentioned in this chapter are by no means the only ones you may be faced with. In chapters that follow we will go into further detail of well-known or scientifically documented steps of the grieving process that you may experience as you try to heal.

KEY TAKEAWAYS

- **Embracing Emotional Realities:** Prepare to journey through uncharted emotional territories, acknowledging that profound grief can lead you to places you never imagined.

- **Forging Your Support Network:** Building a support structure tailored to your needs is an essential step toward finding solace amidst the turmoil.

- **Navigating the Abyss:** Understand that delving into the depths of despair is part of the process, but remember that resilience and seeking help can lead you back to the surface.

- **Shared Sorrows, Shared Healing:** Recognize that your family members are also grappling with grief; coming together in understanding can be a powerful source of healing.

- **Self-Compassion Amidst Guilt:** Be gentle with yourself, releasing any self-blame or guilt that may arise. You've done your best as a parent, and self-compassion is crucial for healing.

- **Carving Paths Beyond Regret:** Accept the irrevocable past, and acknowledge that your choices moving forward can shape your path to healing and growth.

CHAPTER 3
GRIEF IS AN UNSPOKEN LOSS

> "There is a sacredness in tears. They are not the mark of weakness, but of power. They speak more eloquently than ten thousand tongues. They are the messengers of overwhelming grief, of deep contrition, and of unspeakable love."
>
> **Washington Irving (GoodReads, n.d.)**

There are plenty of misconceptions surrounding how people should grieve, how long they should grieve, ways they should behave, what they should or shouldn't be doing. This will differ from one culture to the next and it is our responsibility to respect traditions. If your culture follows specific traditions, you might need to explain them politely or have a close friend or family member do so. So far as traditions are concerned remember there will always be those who are ignorant and may be disrespectful rather than understanding and accepting of how you do things.

Acknowledge that the grief and loss you're experiencing are your own. Only you know how you are feeling, and what you feel is completely different to the way anyone else feels. Your emotions are unique to you as the parent of your child. You might experience the loss intensely, while your spouse may appear cold and distant, trying to hold things together. It may even seem as though they aren't present and experiencing any grief at all.

This behavior may continue for years. It is typical of someone who has still not fully accepted that this trauma is real. However, once it kicks in, tears can flow for a very long time, and mourning suddenly becomes very real. Over the years, those who would have been your support structure may have moved on. You might have one or two close friends who continue to support you. Lean on them whenever needed, and reach out when they contact you or when you're feeling overwhelmed. Allow yourself to experience the emotions that your body is going through. Holding back is what got you into this place of delayed mourning in the first place.

If you find yourself in this category, recognize that it can be especially difficult for you because you chose to go through it alone. There's a strong possibility you may have faced separation or divorce resulting from them distancing yourself from every form of grief. You may have cut yourself off from your spouse and what they were going through at the time leaving them to feel abandoned and having to face the grieving process alone. Who could blame them for feeling deserted especially when they needed someone there. They might have felt as though they were the sole parent responsible for helping other family members work through their grief. As you are reading this, you can understand how due to crossed wires, and misunderstanding about how different and complex individuals can be, there is a disconnect. Sometimes one that becomes permanent.

For clarity, it would be almost cruel to assume for one moment that there is no grieving going on within the spouse despite outward appearances. All that has happened is that every barrier they can possibly put up against any emotion attached to grief and loss has been put up. They have shut off these emotions because they do not want to feel. Essentially, they are afraid of what might happen if they do.

It may be you that is paralyzed with fear of giving into these emotions because you feel they cannot be controlled if you give them space. Instead, you put on a brave facade for those around you. Although you think you can live like this forever, never facing the truth, sometime, somewhere, there will be a trigger. Something will set you off. It may not even be directly related to your child's death. You may never have imagined this would trigger you.

The one thing about losing a child is that other parents who have experienced the same thing will gravitate toward you only to share their own stories. As this begins happening you may be surprised by the number of parents who have experienced what you are trying your best to work through. Allow these people in. Let them share their stories with you. Cry with them. Share your story… These are people you might develop strong connections with through the death of your child. While you may not see them often, they will be the ones sending you a text on the anniversary of your child's death or making a random call when you're having a challenging day.

If you're struggling to cope with your loss and feel that your support group is moving on to help others, which is natural in some cases, it might be time for you to take proactive steps for your own well-being. Perhaps it is time for you to look for a therapist that specializes in grief counseling. Have someone who is reputable refer you. Someone like your General Practitioner. This may be a therapist, or even a grief counseling group in your area that is successful when working with those grieving the loss of a child. You may be questioning whether you even need this, think about what you may get out of it. Even if this means attending one of these meetings.

A therapist will be able to listen to you without judgment. They may provide you with some of the tools you need to cope with what you are feeling. If this is not enough, and your pain and condition warrants further treatment, they may even refer you to seek assistance from a psychiatrist! This should only be if the psychologist believes you need further intervention by someone who can help you with things like severe anxiety, post traumatic stress, and even depression.

Despite thinking that all the psychiatrist is going to do is pump you full of drugs until you are completely numb and further withdrawn from society, the job of a psychiatrist is to determine what effect the trauma has had on your mental health. Too many people are quick to judge when someone is being treated for a mental health condition. What they don't understand is that your psychiatrist and psychologist or therapist will work side-by-side to come up with the best possible treatment plan to get you feeling whole again.

Ignore what others say or the labels they may place on you. The reality is that if you have gone this route you are not only having to work through the loss of your child, you will also have to work through the loss of your marriage, and possibly your other children. Can you see how making this decision when you should be mourning the loss of your child when it happens can create multiple other problems you may have avoided.

Because the support group the therapist has referred you to is one that specializes in working through grief you will suddenly have a platform where you can share your own story. You will be surrounded by individuals each with their own stories and ways they worked through it. Each story will be different. Each coping mechanism may be just as different. You may be inspired to try some of these coping methods for yourself or take several ideas combined. By the time you've been attending for some time you know what your family needs.

Sharing your own story just might be the answer someone else is looking for. Talking about your feelings, and your actual experience aloud in this type of forum can be therapeutic for you. You may discover things about yourself, and your grieving process you never realized or even thought about. Never underestimate the value and positive effect these support groups can have in your life. Something to remember by going to these support groups is that you don't need to rush in and lay your story on the table immediately. You can decide for yourself what you want to share and when.

Let's take a look at the perspective of a spouse who feels the pain of loss immediately. If this is you, you may wonder why you are the only one in your partnership who feels this way. You may want to share these raw emotions with your partner who is just not there yet. All you may receive in return from your spouse is behavior that is indifferent. This can be soul-destroying. You may feel heartbroken, and even betrayed. You don't understand this behavior and may question their commitment. Remember that this is just your perception telling you these things.

Society expects that males should be stoic, strong, and put together to be the rock, and support for the family—not every father is like this. The same can be said of a mother. Sometimes she is the strong one, taking the time to face reality later. Society may expect her to be more compassionate, emotional and caring. Neither of these behaviors are incorrect. It is simply the way individuals work through their grief. You cannot tell how grief is going to be handled by a mother or father. Gender has nothing to do with it.

Based on the book, *Grieving Beyond Gender* by Kenneth Doka, and Terry Martin (2011), there are a number of styles of grief that can possibly be categorized.

These are still just recommendations based on their work as psychiatrists and researchers in this work. It has already been mentioned that there is almost an anticipation and expectation that men and women grieve in certain ways. Each of these are foreseen to be different. It is expected that women be more sensitive, emotional, and in need of encouragement, rather than their counterparts. Males are supposed to be more stoic or braver, putting on that façade, even if it isn't there. They need to be supportive of the needs of the family, especially those who aren't working through their emotions as well as they should.

There is grief that is filled with emotion. Despite this being seen as a feminine trait there are many males that can break down as they are suddenly filled with various types of emotion. Sometimes, this is so stereotyped into a male that a reaction like this seems completely out of place. It is, however, the way they need to find a release and a way to work through their grief. Even getting to the point of acceptance. Remember that you may not necessarily be on the same path as your wife.

Some of the best advice we can offer at this time is to really focus on yourselves, and the rest of your family to strengthen your nucleus. Does this mean that you minimize, or make light of the devastating loss your family have all experienced? This is an emphatic NO! It is just finding some ways to discover coping mechanisms for yourself, and those closest to you, your immediate family. You can perhaps try some of these. You may already know that for yourselves, and your family, some of these methods are simply not going to work.

Work on situations that arise together as a family. By this I am referring to problems, big and small. Break each problem down until they are something that can be handled. Perhaps different members of the family can be allocated certain tasks to do. The timeline can be agreed upon, with a sense of accountability. You may be asking yourself what this has to do with grief. It is one way of looking at such a massive loss in such a way that you can break it down into smaller, more manageable emotions, or outbursts.

You should recognize and accept that grief doesn't need to be one massive thing. It can be divided into a lot of little things that you can manage. You are not taking anything away from these emotions. All you are doing is learning that there are tools out there to help you become more open, and break feelings, and deep-rooted emotions to the front. Another major benefit of this technique is it addresses those feelings of being totally overwhelmed without seeing a way out.

Other ideas include creating lists of information. A great place to start is searching for additional information on your family and your ancestry. This will give you a sense of family, belonging, where you come from, and possibly help with goals to what you want to do yourself, or what kind of legacy you would like to leave for your own family someday. This activity is not just for adults or parents. You can find some really simple only genealogical sites that don't take long to set up your own personal family tree. Be cautious because this can become addictive. Once you begin to dig deeper the more exciting it can become.

Something you may want to do is to leave a heritage by writing something about your loved one on a website specializing in family heritage. One of the ways this can help you work through your grief is that it provides you with something constructive to do. It will still mean facing your loss, but it will put it into perspective, and you are doing something very personal for your deceased loved one. You are processing your grief online, but in a safe space. This is similar to having an online journal. I would like to think that it is safer than your own online journal which might be subject to prying eyes. You may not quite be ready to share your personal journal with them.

- Find solace in your faith and trust the members of your religious community for support.

- Seek assistance from other family members.

- Laugh! Losing a child doesn't mean you can't laugh. It is believed that laughter has the same emotional response as crying. While initially it may feel you are disrespecting your loss. Stop!

Imagine whether your child would want to see you moping around or happy?

- Celebrate the time you shared with them and value both the positive and challenging moments. The good for all the happy memories, and the bad for lessons learned.

- Surround yourself with positive individuals. You have plenty of friends within your circle, including those from work, church, neighbors, and various groups you belong to. Find those that are going to be the most positive and uplifting and spend time with them. You want to feel better by associating with them. Do yourself a favor and try to avoid negative vibes as far as you possibly can.

These are just a couple of ways you can feel better about yourself, and the experience you have recently gone through.

Something to accept is that we will have to face intense grief at some point in our lives. However, I don't think there is a parent in this world who is prepared for the loss of their child. As a parent, it is more or less in our DNA that our children will bury us when we are old and gray. We see each of their lives as long, fulfilled, and happy. We look forward to milestones in each of their lives, right from the time they are born.

We see them going through all the quirks and adolescence. We want that special photo of prom, high school graduation, and possibly watching them receive that college, or university degree. We believe we will try and support them should they decide to travel or leave the nest to live with friends.

We can visualize the magical memories of weddings, all the "I do's." Grandkids to somehow re-energize us when we find ourselves playing with them in the pile of autumn leaves. The home is all abustle with activities over holidays… There are so many things we anticipate when we hold that newborn baby for the very first time. These are the things as a parent we wish for.

Nowhere in this daydream or anticipated life for your child do you see yourself burying them before you. This is possibly one of the most traumatic of all deaths to try and come to terms with, because so often couples, and families who should be there for each other, and supporting one another are so filled with different thoughts and emotions that they aren't present in the moment.

They aren't in synergy, and the last thing is support for one another. There is plenty of blame to go around. This is expressed both inwardly and outward.

There is a complete lack of understanding or even willingness to stop and listen to how other members of the immediate family are feeling, before too much time has gone by, so much irreparable damage has been done that fixing what is now broken is virtually impossible. In this raw and vulnerable state, it is seldom that anyone is prepared to give in either. Each individual is prepared to wallow in their own form of grief. There is no sharing. Communication has broken down, and even when attempted, it appears that this is shut down completely.

So long as nobody is prepared to try, the situation is helpless and hopeless.

Members of the family are quite happy to put blinkers on and a brave face. Most wear masks for others. They pretend they are much stronger than they really are. To the outside world when asked about how they are doing they tell everyone they are fine, almost matter-of-factly, as though nothing had ever happened.

It needs to be understood that this is simply a coping mechanism. As strong as they may be feeling, it will only be a matter of time before it all comes crashing down.

This behavior is actually delayed acceptance. It can happen irrespective of how much time has passed.

OVERLOADED DEATH

Overloaded death brings with it just another style of grief. Having to deal with two or more deaths of people who are close to you within a short period of time can be too much. After losing a child, having to cope with the loss of someone close to you is the next most devastating grief to ever experience. The overload comes because these deaths are close enough, whether in time, or through the relationship to the deceased that your mind and body are completely grief stricken by the loss.

If you are in this situation where things feel like they are getting too much for you, please don't try to do it on your own. Turn to your spouse, those of your genuine friends and family who are aware of your situation, will always be in your corner, having your back.

As if cursed, this actually happened to a friend of ours. While still trying to work through the grief of losing their child it would be a few short months before he was senselessly murdered during a home invasion. For a long time she shut down completely. Losing the two people she loved most in the world within weeks or months of each other was too much for one person to bear. It is times like these when you can try and imagine what you might do in a similar situation. Once again, don't try and console someone like this by saying that you understand where they feel!

The shock of this news was devastating because as parents they shared such a special bond with their daughter. They could speak about her, remember her, and discuss the impact her death had on each of them. His death proved to be almost too much for one person to go through.

When they lost their daughter he had been the anchor holding them together. Now he was suddenly gone without warning. He was the last connection to their child. He was the only person who could fully understand what her death felt like. She would now have to face all these memories and emotions on her own.

Therapy was again necessary to help her figure out how to grieve all over again.

ANTICIPATED DEATH

This is something we haven't touched on too much, but it is also very real. It doesn't mean that because you get time to plan for your child's death. In some ways it is even more difficult because you get to watch your child slowly deteriorate in front of your eyes. There are long goodbyes. Constant uncertainty each time the phone rings. There is the uncertainty that each time you arrive or leave the hospital, or hospice facility, that it will be the last time you see them.

Sure, they know it will someday happen, but living in anticipation affects not just immediate family, the fight to overcome the illness or disease spreads to the community and those that love the individual.

COVID-19 AND DEATH

There's no way to beat around the bush and pretend that this pandemic never happened. It was solely responsible for the deaths of millions of people across all four corners of the globe. I would probably be right in boldly stating that it is highly unlikely that this dreaded disease never negatively affected one family, or individual on the planet in some or other form. Speaking of COVID, this may be included in the section above. The effect it would have on you is beyond words or description. Knowing you cannot be with your child as they desperately fought a disease they had no control over.

When it comes to the death of a child, there could possibly be a cycle of events leading up to their death that parents the world over will replay each step again and again, asking themselves over and over whether had scenarios or choices been different, could their child have survived?

- What if they took that fever a little more seriously?

- Paid more attention to that cough?

- Listened to what their child was saying when they described aches and pains instead of chalking it up to how they normally behaved

These and so many other questions can plague parents who lost a child or even children to this devastating virus. Parents who were forced to say their farewells through technology. Video chats, and other platforms supporting video and audio live streaming. All parents could do was stand by and watch their child deteriorate in front of their eyes, treated by staff wearing so much personal protective gear making all those science fiction movies seem mild in comparison.

The greatest challenge was the inability to be there in person. Once their child had passed on, they knew the process of dealing with the bodies of Covid victims. Hospitals were overwhelmed, overextended without the capacity to work with the sheer volume of the dead. Mortuaries were full, funeral homes could not provide enough coffins, crematoriums ran full steam. It would take unprecedented demands on those working the front lines. Something only coming to light long after the world began to pick up the semblance of pieces, and rebuild the world.

These deaths of children were harrowing to parents who grieved in a way that couldn't be compared with any other loss. Unable to say goodbye. Unable to hold for one last time, caress a face, shed a tear over a body, be free to possibly have a variety of coffins to choose from rather than being forced to accept the choice of disposal of remains dictated by suits in boardrooms. To them it was simply a clinical decision, to you, it was the final resting place that your child deserved. Being forced to accept the inevitable was a completely different kind of hurt.

For those more fortunate it would still mean waiting for funeral plots, or a place in line at a crematorium. Each delay would extend and postpone the grieving process. For many the choice would be a simple memorial service attended by a handful of close friends and relatives as dictated by the limitations of this virus.

Memorial services would be broadcast to friends and others prepared to sacrifice some time to offer support. Yet, they were unable to provide that physical touch, a final hug to hold in your heart forever. The pain of having all rights of any physical interaction whatsoever could cause a totally different kind of grief.

Mourning this kind of loss would redefine an historic era of trying to work through the loss of a child to a virus that the world had no control over and what seemed like never-ending gloom. For these parents the sun had set over their child. They felt helpless. Lockdown isolated them from the world. It was often a catalyst to extreme depression for either or both parents in certain homes. The breakdown of entire family units often hung in the balance.

If any type of death could epitomize this era in history, it would be this. Help would finally be available as restrictions were lifted. As a parent this would haunt you for the rest of your life. It is also understandable if you feel as though you had been robbed of the dignity owed you.

The mention of this is done in memory of each and every child that died as a result of a relentless disease, and those parents for their unprecedented sacrifice as they tried to navigate a journey they never signed up for.

In most instances, there are final goodbyes from all members of the family. Even vigils were held. Extended family members and even friends can visit and extend their love.

Not to make this experience less painful or as devastating—there is a time period when you know what is going to happen rather than simply having your child snatched away without warning.

KEY TAKEAWAYS

- It is okay to mourn; in fact, it is better than holding back your emotions.

- Seek support from others and consider joining grief support groups.

- Sharing your story can have a profound impact and provide help to others.

- The pain of losing a child is profound, regardless of the circumstances—whether due to cancer or Covid, these situations are equally devastating.

- Don't let others diminish or undermine the magnitude of what you are experiencing.

CHAPTER 4
SAILING BEYOND GRIEF: REBUILDING, RECONNECTING, AND HONORING PRECIOUS LEGACIES

> *"It's so curious; one can resist tears and 'behave' very well in the hardest hours of grief. But then someone makes you a friendly sign behind a window, or one notices that a flower that was in bud only yesterday has suddenly blossomed, or a letter slips from a drawer… and everything collapses."*
> **Colette (What's Your Grief, 2019)**

When grief happens normally, there are a range of emotions that happen to you either physically or emotionally… Depending on the circumstance, you may feel completely numb, weak in the knees, or your limbs may feel heavier than before. You may be overcome by crying (occasionally hysterically). And then… unable to stop no matter how much anyone tries to console you. It is not unusual for you to feel nauseous. Your heart may race, and you might feel like someone is sitting on your chest and you are unable to breathe.

These are just a few of the physical things you may go through when experiencing such a loss. Watch for similar signs through other members of your family too. Sometimes we get so caught up in our own grief that we forget that we are not the only ones experiencing the loss. This is where support and healing for the entire family begins.

In the coming days, it's important to grant yourself forgiveness if confusion about what is happening around you. You may even believe you are seeing or hearing the person. If you are more forgetful of common things, you aren't losing your mind, it is merely a normal side effect of trying to process what has happened in your life.

A significant aspect to consider is how our emotions influence our experience. These emotions can influence both our behavior, and physical responses. They may even amplify the feelings you already have, making them that much harder to deal with.

Emotionally we move through some of the typical steps of grief, while there are many more emotions, we feel that are undefined yet undeniably there. This is not to say that everyone will follow these same patterns. They may feel all of these… or just a handful. It may happen all at once, one at a time, quite randomly.

Experiencing initial anger, whether directed at God, the situation (especially if someone else was involved, or as a result of nature—something you really had no control over.) You may be angry with yourself, and decisions made that day. It's crucial to acknowledge that directing anger during this time may hinder healing. It will not change anything, other than making it much more difficult to come to terms with the situation and bring yourself to a place where you can find peace.

You may feel like there's no point in living, so you choose to just go with the flow and motions of life. You can't seem to bring yourself to do the things you used to do with vigor and zest. If you have other children, they become victims to your lackluster demeanor. They bear the brunt of you feeling indifferent about what is going on around you because you can't see your way through. The only way to approach this is by working your way through the pain. This may be challenging at first, but recognition that you have an entire family that needs you, and your support—especially now, is a start.

One of the unhealthiest places to be is to deny that any of it has happened. When you battle to accept or refuse to accept that your child is dead. Typical of this scenario is insisting that your child is away and will walk through the doors at any moment. It is living in a dream. Forcing yourself to accept what has taken place over the past few days as though it were a dream and creating your own reality. When it comes to this emotion, there will come a time when the dream ends. What was once something you experienced and lived through before, becomes something you need to face yet again.

Having a short temper or becoming more irritable with those around you can become understandable, and even forgivable. It is when you take it beyond an accepted period of time (the mourning phase), that this might present as a problem. Having said this though, we have also mentioned that the duration of mourning is completely different for everyone. Explaining this to others can lead to a level of acceptance where your behavior becomes more tolerable.

The following emotion of loneliness can be experienced by any member of the family who was exceptionally close to the deceased. In any family, there will be one member where a child will gravitate toward. Whether a mother, father, or sibling—the bond between the two is undeniably strong. Emotionally, it will feel like there's a piece of you that's missing. Your best friend is gone, leaving a gaping hole of loneliness that to them right now, seems impossible to fill. They may even withdraw within themselves feeling entirely on their own despite being surrounded by those that can help support you through the emotions you are experiencing.

Among the most challenging emotions, particularly within families, is the tendency to assign blame on someone else's shoulders. These often occur with the sentence of "If only you had…" or "they had," "she had," and even "I had." It can take a long time to get over these feelings of guilt and anger, and even anger directed toward something, or someone else. The truth is that what's done is done. No matter how much finger-pointing, or making senseless accusations, nothing is going to change. The outcome will not change.

Dealing with numbness is complex and requires thoughtful consideration. This will possibly last until there's acceptance. One thing is for certain, there are so many great things in life happening around you that you are possibly missing out on because you are choosing not to recognize them because you insist on feeling a sense of detachment from those around you. It's times like this where you become cut-off from those who love you the most. Those who have experienced exactly what you have experienced. The only thing that is different however is if we have chosen to work through the pain.

While this may sound cruel to some, perhaps you are experiencing relief when your child leaves. These emotions usually occur when there is a forewarning that your child is terminally ill, has a severe deformity, or a life-threatening disease. We have already spoken of the painstaking hours and hours spent at your child's bedside not knowing when you will either receive that call or have them simply drift off while holding your hand. For parents and family members going through this, they may feel a sense of relief. Relief that their child is no longer in pain.

When a child's passing is abrupt, shock becomes an inevitable part of the journey. This is the body doing its best to help you process what is happening, what has just happened, and how your life will never be the same ever again. You perhaps feel as though your life is shattered. Your family unit is completely shattered. It is only once you have overcome the shock that reality can begin to set in.

DEATH'S EFFECT ON RELATIONSHIPS

It would be ideal to assure you that relationships will remain perfect. That people will support you, and you will be grateful for their willingness to help. You will rely on their kindness for a while, and all will go swimmingly! Not so. As mentioned throughout to this point, you will experience a definite shift in relationships. This shift will range from blame to anger, rage, or total withdrawal and shutting off from the world. Those around who have never experienced this for themselves find it difficult to process or understand. How can they? They have no idea of any of the emotions swimming through your head constantly.

Emotions of bitterness might result in turning away even the most well-meaning, and closest of friends. Some of these relationships might be mended while others may be damaged beyond repair.

Among the most heart-wrenching outcomes is when couples find it impossible to navigate the loss. Patterns of blame occur. Cracks begin to form that were never there or aren't actually there—it just perceives to be. The relationship reaches a point of no return and ends in divorce. When there seems to be no coming back from the experience, families are broken apart…

For couples on their own this option seems much easier because there's nothing really to lose, other than each other, but this changes substantially when children are involved. It is worse for them. They are already dealing with all the emotions of loss of a sibling, now, as parents, you are throwing divorce in the mix. Many of these children simply cannot bear all these emotions and begin to play up, getting involved in the wrong crowd. They become the statistic of those children who feel abandoned, lost, unloved, and lonely.

Parents begin to wonder what went wrong. They question their parenting skills, and once again point fingers at their ex-partner. Seldom do each of these parents actually look at themselves in the mirror or search inward to find the real catalyst was the emotional damage they put their children through at the time of loss—a time when the family should have really been supporting each other and helping each other find coping mechanisms that worked for each individually.

Sadly, divorce in a time of an additional crisis leads to problems in our children as they move through adolescence. They search for where they belong, trying to find their feet as they are constantly shifted between parents every other week and on holidays. Due to this, they seldom get the chance to rely on parents to work through the mourning process with them. Parents are normally too wrapped up in what's happening with them to take their children's emotional health into account. What they don't realize is that they could be causing their child a lifetime of emotional damage.

Undoubtedly, friendships may also experience strain as you navigate your emotions of what has just happened. If you had children of similar ages, they may begin feeling uncomfortable around you—not wanting to open wounds and get your mind racing again.

Others may have meant well and not been received as well as expected. Feelings may have been hurt and emotional ego's may have been bruised. Neither party will give in to it, admitting the possibility of it being their fault and so friendships could be lost.

A challenging situation arises when external family members inadvertently contribute to the cycle of emotional turmoil. Perhaps they overstep the boundaries, all the time meaning well. Perhaps they say the wrong thing, right at the wrong time. There could be hundreds of reasons why external families fall into this category. These relationships can normally be mended, it takes time and forgiveness.

TIPS FOR SUPPORTING EACH OTHER

Consider these suggestions as potential coping mechanisms to explore. Not all of them will be for you but you really won't know until you give them a go. Before you pooh pooh them, think about how you and your family are currently hurting and how some of these methods may be of value.

BE THERE FOR ONE ANOTHER

This means being fully present for them. Take the time to really listen. Don't offer your opinion or advice midway through their story. Remember that this is the way they perceive things and may not be your own. Pay attention to how they are feeling. What behavior or emotion they are displaying, be supportive of those. Don't expect their emotions or feelings of grief, and loss to change overnight. Remember that these relationships have been forming from the day the child was born.

Even in the case of infant death, the parents have been looking forward to this wonderful new life in their home. They would have painstakingly been planning from the day they first discovered they were expecting. Don't for one moment minimize this or think this is any less important than the death of a teen. Loss is loss, regardless of age, and should be treated that way.

When your partner or member of the family is feeling especially low. Give them time to talk if that's what they want. Perhaps they want to be left alone in their thoughts in quiet reflection or contemplation. Give them their space.

If you really want to help them, don't ask them to "snap out of it" because you believe it has been long enough for them to still be grieving. Making that statement is possibly one of the most hurtful things to say to someone who is grieving.

You cannot determine how long it will take you to come to terms with your loss. In most instances, those who have lost a child will think about them each day for the rest of their lives. It is the intensity of those thoughts that may determine the outer display of feelings of loss.

WRITING OR DRAWING

I have mentioned writing instead of journaling because writing covers a much broader spectrum. For smaller siblings, drawing can be a great activity. Writing might include things like journaling your feelings, without being afraid of having to open up to anyone.

This is one place where you can be completely honest about how you really feel about your loss.

You can attribute blame if that's the direction you want to go. You can take your anger and frustrations out on God.

Perhaps you want to discuss the more painful, and personal side of grief. Write about those places you find yourself gravitating toward when you least expect it.

You may want to write your loved one a letter. This may contain all the things you wish you had told them if they were still here. Perhaps it describes all the ways you were proud of them—the hopes and dreams you had for them had they been alive. These letters may remain exactly where they are in your journal, or you may want to burn them.

In most instances, these are something extremely personal and chances are you will be reluctant to share those with others.

Encourage your children to do the same.

If they are still too young to write, have them draw a picture, or pictures of what they felt their sibling represented to them. There are many ways these can be honored. Give your child the option of what they would like to do with the picture. Perhaps they want it next to their bed where they can always remember. They may want to join you in burning their drawing.

BUILDING A ROCK GARDEN—FOR YOUNGER KIDS

Another activity for younger children is building a rock garden in a quiet place in your garden. This could be added to for each birthday, special holiday, or special event in your lost child's life. Allow your younger children to choose and place each rock. As they become older, they will begin to appreciate the significance of what they have done and by then it would have become a ritual for the family. It is also one way to help your entire family to honor your loved one.

We feel that this next exercise is something more poignant with long lasting effects, one where the whole family can participate, not just initially, but throughout the lifespan. It will leave a legacy someday. Find a tree indigenous to your territory. Look for a sapling that is hardy and can thrive under most environmental conditions. Where possible, decide on the young plant together as a family. Involve everyone in deciding where the young tree should be planted, as well as the planting process. Family members can alternate caring for the tree, i.e., watering it, sweeping dead leaves as seasons change. This will be a memory tree, planted especially in memory of your loved one. It will be a constant reminder for everyone, without anyone having to be overly creative.

HONOR THEM AND THEIR MEMORY

When family holidays come around it can be a confusing time for everyone. Do you do something to remember them or to honor them, or do you pretend that everything is fine and you carry on as a family that will never be the same again?

Sustain their memory. Honor their presence. Celebrate their birthdays as cherished milestones. A friend of mine lost her daughter when she was just a few days old. Each year on her birthday she bakes and professionally decorates an age appropriate cake to celebrate a life that might have been. At midnight as her birthday comes around, she will waken her other two boys and her husband and as a family, they celebrate the blessing she was for them.

At Christmas time, there are baubles with her name on them, a special stocking just for her. I'm not suggesting that you have to follow this example. Find your own way to remember. The main thing is not to be afraid to even speak their name.

TRY MEDITATION

Extend this practice to the entire family. You can teach your children from a young age that a certain amount of time spent alone in your thoughts, reading, writing in a journal, listening to soothing music, or just sitting thinking deeply, has strong benefits to you as an individual. It can help you become grounded, more focused on what life has to offer and often more grateful for everything you already have.

Whichever way you cut it, looking for creative ways to work through deep emotions of loss can be extremely important for families to stick together. They provide you with the opportunity to draw strength from one another when needed. You can learn to spend quality time together remembering your loved one in a positive way.

KEY TAKEAWAYS

* **Emotional Complexity:** Grief encompasses a range of emotions, often influenced by external factors. Recognizing this complexity can help you navigate the grieving process more effectively.

* **Relationship Dynamics:** Grief can impact relationships, but your choices determine whether they strengthen or falter. Your actions have the power to mend and rebuild connections or contribute to their deterioration.

* **Rebuilding and Honoring:** Consider ways to rebuild your family and home while honoring the memory of your lost child. Support each other and embrace individual differences. Express your thoughts and feelings through writing or other means that resonate with you.

* **Children's Grief:** Acknowledge that your children are also grieving. Involve them in commemorating their sibling and listen to their ideas, as their perspectives can offer insights and contribute to a sense of peace.

CHAPTER 5

JOURNEY OF THE HEART: NAVIGATING THE PHASES OF GRIEF

> *"Everyone grieves in different ways. For some, it could take longer or shorter. I do know it never disappears. An ember still smolders inside me. Most days, I don't notice it, but, out of the blue, it'll flare to life."*
> **Maria V. Snyder (2013/2014)**

By experiencing these intense and amplified emotions of loss, you're already aware that they can often occur simultaneously. The impact of this loss may linger for a considerable period. You know that life has to go on. This may take months or even years to get to this point. Indeed, certain triggers will evoke memories of your child. A certain song, places you would go to regularly just on your own or even as a family. It may be the family's favorite pizza joint, a coffee shop where you would get fresh muffins or bagels for breakfast. These memories and moments of mourning may arise unexpectedly. They will also begin to ease over time. While these memories will endure, and you may even share them with friends on occasion, the saying 'time heals all wounds' finds relevance in this context.

It's challenging to convey the stark contrast between the emotions of losing and mourning your own child, compared to the feelings associated with losing a close friend or adult family member.

A lot of this is because we know deep down, the family member has most likely lived their lives hopefully to the fullest. You have known them, although not intimately unless it is a spouse, in which case your type of bereavement and mourning process will also be different.

Observe that there isn't a singular way to grieve; it defies a one-size-fits-all formula. That's why so many parents feel that overwhelming sense of failure, and an urgency to be better. They need to do better, even if it is the couple's only child. This is when it hurts the most. The attention that was once devoted to your child now leaves an emptiness. There's no more activities, play dates, other supporters, overall, just that busyness of life. You have purpose as a parent regardless of which role you take.

What can be particularly painful, and have a more profound impact, is if you were working full-time while your child was young, or at the time of their passing. You might find yourself haunted by the choice you made, carrying it with you throughout your life. Irrespective of your financial circumstances. The weight of not being there when they needed you. Simply showing them how important they were, and how much you loved them would have gone such a long way to ease some of these steps of grief we are going to talk about in this chapter.

There are five major steps of grief that are referred to so often that most people can already identify with what they are, namely: denial, anger, bargaining, depression, and finally acceptance. Almost like a maze within a maze, for each of these stages of grief come their own sets of problems and challenges. Looking at all the stages of grief is enough to make even a normal individual terrified (without having gone through any harrowing ideal).

The goal is to have the tools at your disposal to work through each of these stages, effectively trying to convey some ideas of how to deal with these situations as they arise. Without attempting something constructive that has the potential to help you there's a strong chance that you will spiral out of control.

When it comes to losing a child, the emotion and experience is right up there with one of the most earth shattering and devastating experiences anyone could have to go through in their lives. There's no question about thoughts and emotions you are feeling then and they can easily turn into depression and anxiety as a result of the trauma you have gone through.

While you may be thinking we are simply compiling this list on our own, it was first discovered in 1967. Called the *Social Readjustment Rating Scale*, or the *Holmes-Rahe Stress Scale*, it indicates what are known today as life stressors. The number of these events experienced within the same year and accumulated, is what can lead to mental breaks and other health problems (Mind Tools Content Team, 2023).

This scale, perhaps because it was first developed more than half a century ago, is debated by many. Reasons given are that other factors come into play as these stressful situations occur. For the purpose of us moving forward, listing these stressors is worthwhile and you can make your own conclusion as to whether this list could potentially lead to physical or mental disease of some description.

These major stressors according to an article on *Life Stressors* (Kubala, 2022) include:

STAGES OF GRIEF

As we go through each of the five stages of grief, we are going to look at:

- When they occur
- How they occur
- How to deal with them when they occur

Using them to benefit you further in your healing process as you grieve. Using the combination of healing and grieving may sound like they are at polar opposites, and they are really… but, healing requires you to navigate the grieving process. Notice I said "through," not around, over, under, or any other way to magically move from one very deep, dark, hollow, place where all you want to do is either join your child or simply give up, to the ultimate of the five stages of grief. Arriving at acceptance, in whatever form it takes for you, demands a willingness to progress step by step, placing one foot in front of the other. Before unpacking each of the stages of grief, gaining insight into the origins and history of these stages could prove beneficial.

It was a brilliant psychiatrist, Elisabeth Kübler-Ross who discovered there were different phases one would go through when trying to process overwhelming grief. This was in 1969, and her hypothesis still stands today. According to her, you are looking at:

- Denial
- Anger
- Bargaining
- Depression
- Acceptance

In this chapter we will cover each of these steps. Be aware that these steps have the potential to harm us as well as help us. Not physically, but emotionally, and this could be more painful, and more difficult to work through. Our approach to the phase you are facing needs to be positive so you can recognize other positive sides to each phase. They all have something you can tap into that can help you work through your grief. Understand from the get-go that nothing is a quick fix or one day cure. It is a process. A journey you will embark on, without knowing when or where your final destination will be.

Another thing worth mentioning is that these cycles are fluid rather than linear. This means that while Kübler-Ross may have them in this order, you may not experience denial before anger or acceptance finally. Throughout your grieving process for the rest of your life, you need to be aware of each of these so you can apply techniques and tools for each. There are five cycles. Because you are going through the most painful grief of all, look at these as merely reference points. Yes, they come across as being ordered and a process that makes logical sense for you to experience however, they are simply a reference point. A starting point for you to understand where you are. Understanding each step gives you the advantage of using the resources for that step.

You may only identify with one or two of these steps. At the same time, having experienced severe trauma you may go through exactly the same process a couple of times before you can put everything to bed. This may be two or three times working on one single stage of grief.

Let's take a look at each of these from the book, On Death and Dying (Kübler-Ross & Byock, 1969/2014) which has acted as a guide to working through the trauma of death for more than a century.

Taking each of these into context, they are all pretty strong emotions. Negative ones, but that's where you are at. Your loss has transformed your experience from simply going through each day to merely trying to survive. These emotions are ones we may typically feel when losing a child. We may feel some of these at the time our child dies. We may not feel any of them at all (which is in fact denial).

DENIAL

Denial prevents you from feeling the pain of losing your loved one. You see the entire situation as a dream. It hasn't happened. Your child is going to return to you and life will go on as though nothing has happened. You anticipate a message on your mobile device. You expect them to cry after a midday or midnight nap. This is where you would typically keep their room spick and span, without anything out of place so when they come back everything will be exactly the same.

You deny that it is your child when first hearing the news. It cannot be, there has been a mistake, you are still not satisfied even identifying or seeing your child's lifeless body. This denial is a hollowness and an overwhelmingly intense heartbreak. You feel like you cannot breathe, whether it is that you cannot, or don't really want to breathe anymore still needs to be determined.

During this denial process some individuals may experience what they perceive as being real visions of their child. They see them everywhere. In a crowd, in their favorite park, even in the walls of their own home. Why I say 'individuals' is that it is not necessarily both couples. These hallucinations are in a dream-like state. This is a coping mechanism so they don't have to accept their loss right then. So long as these hallucinations occur, they feel there's a chance for them to gladly be able to trade places by sacrificing their own lives for their child. For just a moment, there is hope! The only problem is that this is not real and at some stage there needs to be a realization of that.

ANGER

Each of the steps of grief form a system to support how you are feeling at different times. When anger is involved you can become angry at the world, angry at God, angry at your partner, your other siblings, and anyone else you can possibly find to lay the blame on. The only thing about being angry is that we always lash out at the wrong people and for the wrong reasons. There is not a single benefit to being angry. All it does is make us bitter.

The problem with being angry all the time, especially when dealing with or blaming your partner, has the very real possibility of costing you your relationship. It's when separation and divorce may occur unless the anger can be dealt with. One single emotion attached to grief can create another life-changing experience not only for each of you as a couple, but for your children and other loved ones. You may not see it at the time but there are many around you that are doing their best to intervene to help you keep your marriage intact. If you are so angry you may be so harsh with them that they also withdraw, leaving you totally alone.

With divorce, instead of dealing with one loss in terms of losing a child, there is a second loss that is irreparable and often one of deep regret and remorse later in life. More often than not it is too little too late.

If only you get to recognize that it is the pain of losing your child that is causing you to be so angry, you can work through it—as pain, instead of anger. This is when this emotion can help you begin to heal. Admit to yourself and those closest to you, that you are hurting. That the loss is causing you severe pain and the only way you know of dealing with that pain at the moment is through anger. It is a pain you don't know how to process. The first step is admitting you are hurting. You can get help for pain. What you really need are coping skills. Ways to direct your anger in healthy ways, and even techniques that can help calm and heal you. Things that can bring you peace instead of heartache.

BARGAINING

Bargaining falls under another stage of grief. You find yourself spiraling into this stage whenever you find yourself trying to make some sense of it all. You question your own power and ability in your child's death. None of this is helpful. It just leads to you feeling even more sad. Sad within yourself. Sad about the situation. Sad for your family, you get the idea. The sense of sadness engulfs you completely. Bargaining with someone means negotiation in some way and being prepared to sacrifice something for what some might term 'the greater good'.

In most instances this bartering and negotiating is with us internally. We go through all those motions of questioning your role or behavior in what happened or led to the death of your child.

Sabrina Romanoff a psychologist has described this phase of the grieving process as:

> Bargaining is a defense against the feelings of helplessness experienced after a loss. It happens when people struggle to accept the reality of the loss and the limits of their control over the situation (Gupta, 2022).

We've already discussed how you can go through those phases of asking all those "what if questions." You lay blame at your own feet; you try to bargain with that higher power. You don't want to continue feeling the way you do.

Bargaining can present itself in a number of different ways, but most involve negative feelings toward yourself. Whether you are carrying guilt, anguish, insecurities, overwhelm, and overthinking about what has happened. These and other feelings similar to these seem to be constant, however, there are various things you can be doing instead of holding onto something that can't be changed and you really have no control over.

Take time for healing. Come to terms with yourself that you aren't going to feel the same immediately after your loss. It is not surprising if you ever return to how you felt before the event. Because a part of you has died, that can never be replaced no matter how hard you try and would desperately dream for it to change.

A lot of bargaining happens both past and present. In the past because of wanting your actions leading up to the event to be different, and the present for the strength to be able to move forward feeling better about yourself than you possibly do now. Of course, nobody wants to feel regret, guilt, shame, or other negative emotions for an extended period of time. There must be some way to begin to find peace and feel better.

Working through this means you need to pay attention to:

REMEMBERING AND REHASHING THE PAST

There is nothing to be gained from this. What is done is done and you can never reshape what has happened in the past, all you can do is turn to acceptance (the last in our grief cycle).

JOURNAL

We have briefly mentioned the power of journaling your thoughts. This is yet another time when you should be taking pen to paper and recording all the negative emotions you are experiencing. This can often place your feelings and emotions into perspective. It can also help you identify where most of your energy is going. If you can see that your thoughts and emotions are futile, where you can do nothing about the original situation it can make coming to terms with it much quicker.

REACH OUT FOR HELP

At any stage within the grief cycle you feel you really aren't doing so well on your own, or even with the loving support of your family, it may be time to reach out for help. Rather than going into a deep depression where you find yourself with no will to live or spend your time in bed in an attempt to process your grief, look for a reputable registered mental health practitioner.

There are also many support groups in your area. It's worthwhile looking at joining one of these because everyone is fighting the same battle.

Perhaps they have managed to move past bargaining and onto another point in the grieving cycle. They can help you by pointing you in the right direction to make adjustments to your life to support what you need to do.

If this cycle of grief is not broken by moving forward quickly enough it leads directly on to the next cycle.

I'd like to remind you that the five stages of grief aren't linear, and it doesn't mean that because they have been defined as such by Elisabeth Kübler-Ross. The method with only five stages to it is the one those in the psychological profession use.

DEPRESSION

Many of the points we have already discussed can lead to depression if left long enough. You may now realize that nothing you do will change the past. Some of the previous methods tried have realized that each of these steps lead to the result. Sadness and feeling emptiness inside. There are times when you feel helpless and hopeless. You ask yourself what the point is of carrying on. The past event feels more real now than ever before. Your emotions are heightened, and you experience all aspects of the emotional pain of your loss more deeply than before.

You can't control your thoughts or where your mind is going. All you do know is feel an emptiness and sadness you can't shake off. You don't know how. You can't seem to do much at all because being able to function is a challenge. You no longer have the energy to fight all of the emotions that seem to be coming at you from all directions. So much so that you hit rock bottom. You freeze up. No longer able to cope or to function. You can't see a way out. Everything seems surrounded by a dense fog. It is darkness, and a sense of impending doom. Hopelessness and helplessness overtake your mind and at this stage you may even begin to lose your will to live.

Depression hits the whole family. You are of no use to anyone, When you are depressed you have no energy to fight off all the emotions you are feeling. One thing to remember is that depression can look completely different from one person to another.

For some it is a deep sadness and having a lack of energy or motivation to do anything. This may be diagnosed as depression, severe anxiety disorder (SAD), or post traumatic stress disorder (PTSD). You may be surprised by the possible diagnosis of PTSD. You shouldn't be. What you and your family have experienced is a trauma and a serious one. Losing your child is not something you can just shrug off and continue with your day-to-day life pretending that all is fine in the world. Whatever your diagnosis though, don't give in to accepting the way society labels these conditions. Remember that it is not them that are currently standing in your shoes.

Giving yourself permission to mourn, grief, cry, sometimes even shouting as loud as you can gives you the freedom from the emotions you are currently feeling. There may be loads of emotions you are trying to work through. Many you have never experienced before because of the exceptionally close bond you shared between you and your child. Irrespective, it is a bond that you believed could never be broken and now they are gone. Just try and work through each motion one at a time. Be sure you can come to some finality with that emotion and move on to the next. Don't go so deep into any one emotion that you become stuck there.

For many parents this state is just temporary, while others never really recover, not completely at least. Accept during this step, and each of the others, that some triggers may occur at any time. Sometimes within days or months, or even years later that can send you right back into the same depressed or even worse depressed state.

ACCEPTANCE

The final step in the grief process when losing a child is being able to eventually accept they are gone. They won't be walking back through the front door. You will no longer hear their car engine pulling into the drive, or their chatter and dirty handprints all over the walls. You now feel sorry for forcing them to clean off the marks—with a bit of help of course. You will no longer enjoy that brand new baby smell as you gently rock them to sleep in the middle of the night or sit with them in the hospital, just waiting for news of test results.

Going through each of these steps can help you take your time to work through what you have gone through. You can slowly begin to heal. We have just scratched the surface when it comes to things in each of the steps you may need to work through. As you do though, you will discover for yourself that you are not imagining things. That your loss is real. You may begin to feel some raw emotions. Ones you need to work through.

When mentioning that these are fluid, you might go through any of these emotions a number of times in the healing process so you can begin to move forward.

There are hundreds of different circumstances that may describe the way you lost your child, what matters most is that you have been able to work through those of the steps of grief you needed to in order for you to come to this point. Even being accepting can quickly bounce between other stages of grief. Once you understand this you can be more forgiving toward yourself and other members of your family.

A lot of this happens when all the bouquets are dead, when you've finally decided to pack away all the bereavement cards. When there are no more friends simply popping in as a means of checking up to see how you are. In short, your support group that was slowly dwindling is now completely silent, or they've moved on to some other cause.

The only real support you are and should be receiving is from your partner, your children (if they are old enough to understand exactly what is happening) and possibly some of your extended family members.

You will perhaps find your continued attendance to your bereavement support group the only other place where you feel comfortable discussing your feelings and listening to the stories of others, because more often than not they are similar to your own. Members of this group are experiencing the same pain, and you never know who you are helping by being there either.

As part of these steps of grief, because processing it or going through these emotions are different for everyone, the loss of a child can result in marriage partners turning against each other. Often being scathing, ugly, and hurtful. This is really just the hurt talking, but so often this is too late to realize and marriages dissolve when couples should be spending time talking to one another about their feelings and emotions. It can be years before individuals realize that a snap decision changed the trajectory of their lives completely.

Although there are these five stages of grief that have been listed and they are in the order they were originally set out. You may say that they are technically correct. Any one of these has the potential to make or break you. The most important message is that you as the individual who is experiencing this loss needs to identify the coping mechanism that works for you. Hold onto it. Work through it because remember that it is only through that you can reach healing on the other side. Irrespective of what you are going through if you have an immediate family unit, you may need to be considerate of their needs as well, rather than being selfish in placing your desires before theirs. However, these emotions and considerations need to be reciprocated. What I am trying to say is that you need to be in this healing process together. The only way to achieve this is through open lines of communication.

Healing takes time, and you need to be kind to yourself and understanding of those around you that really matter.

KEY TAKEAWAYS

- There are five key stages of grief. Each carries different emotions that can range in intensity. These are denial, anger, bargaining, depression, and acceptance.

- They are not linear, meaning you won't necessarily follow the steps or patterns as laid out.

- Be as prepared as you can be and expect changes in your own life and those of your loved ones. Communicate openly especially before you withdraw.

- Be kind to yourself, understanding that healing takes time. You have to work through it to come out the other side.

- No matter what you settle on, you need to realize and accept that nothing will bring your loved one back. This is possibly the last thing you want to hear.

CHAPTER 6
MENDING SHATTERED PIECES: HEALING AMIDST LOSS AND TURMOIL

> "We all want to do something to mitigate the pain of loss or to turn grief into something positive, to find a silver lining in the clouds. But I believe there is real value in just standing there, being still, being sad."
> **John Green (Luc, 2021)**

When a child is suddenly taken away from you it is difficult to imagine you and your life will ever be whole again. To answer this question, or intense emotion you may be feeling, no, there is no way to replace the child you have lost. Your remaining children and family members will be experiencing loss, often completely different from your own. This may mean you fix the fracture in your family dynamic. It's not as easy as trying to hold things together with an emotional band-aid, where you treat it as a "one-size fits all."

No family is the same. As a parent you may be faced with all the other emotions that have already been mentioned. You are now turning to the rest of your family to do your best to repair the damage to your family unit. Children may be withholding their real emotions because they don't want to burden you as a parent. Because they are so close, they can see what's happening firsthand. The reality is that they can only hold things together for so long. It is also unfair of you, as a parent, to expect them to be more "together" than you.

It is time for you, or together with your spouse to take them aside and have a genuine, yet frank discussion with them. Find out where they are when it comes to mourning. Let them open up completely. If they are being strong for your sake let them know it is their time to release all the emotions they have been holding back.

The healing now needs to be for the entire family. If you have been holding back on discussing anything to do with your child who has died, this is maybe the first thing that needs to be addressed. You need to talk through how each of you feel about it. Discuss it openly. Just like you would share in a grieving session within a counseling group, do the same thing with your children in an open forum. Let them share some of the raw emotions they may be facing. Perhaps they are having nightmares, are battling through panic attacks whenever they leave home or are even withholding feelings of depression. You may think that depression is something that each parent will pick up quickly. Even the most astute parent can miss this if a child wants to keep this hidden.

You may be smothering your children in your attempt to keep them safe. This might include things like refusing that they leave the house at certain times, or incorporating all sorts of rules within the home as a parent just wanting to keep your other children safe. You need to know that even the most protected children can still be prone to fatalities. Accepting that we don't have control over everything that happens in our lives or the lives of our family is possibly one of the most valuable lessons you can learn at this time.

WHAT MIGHT BE BROKEN

It's important to take care of your own health and mental health to stand tall for each of your other children to help them with the coping mechanisms they may need. Whether you need to attend therapy as a family unit or make appointments with psychiatrists to help a child who is battling depression, you need to be an adult and make the tough decisions.

Watch your other children for silent grief. This is when they really are grieving deep inside but don't want to place any further pressure on you. They can see what you are going through, and yes, they get to say they do understand what you are going through. Their mourning will also be as individual as each of them are. They each have different relationships with their siblings. What one sees as devastating may not be as heartbreaking for another. The feelings of what was left unsaid or the way things were left will continue to plague them for years to come.

As parents, it is not enough thinking that because they are still a child they don't really understand and they will get over it. Think about how you felt when others told you to "simply get over it." You were beyond angry. Your surviving child will feel exactly the same way. On top of this, they don't have the emotional intelligence or life-skills to be able to work through the death of a loved one, no matter how together you may think they are. Even in the event of an expected death, there's nothing automatic about how a sibling will feel about it. They may have expected to feel one way, only to be faced with completely different emotions when they lost their sibling.

HELPING CHILDREN

You may believe that everything above covers all the emotions and fears your surviving children may be experiencing. It is easy for them to fall into a category known as "forgotten mourners." This can easily occur within your home if all the attention and especially support from others are directed at parents. Children often come second or third or who knows how far down the list. It should be a priority that this doesn't happen in your home. Surviving children should never fall through the cracks.

Their emotions may be even stronger or more complex than those of you or your spouse. Many times they may be afraid of the same thing happening to them, or another loved one in their immediate family. This will cause them to behave differently. A lot of this can be resolved by setting up open lines of communication. Give your children complete access to you at any time, without reservation or becoming aggravated. You may feel this way because the same emotions keep being raised. Don't show this frustration, instead, use it as a unique learning opportunity for you to draw much closer to your surviving children.

They may be experiencing survivor's guilt where they, very much like you, would give anything to have sacrificed themselves in place of the deceased child/sibling. Because it is something you have been feeling you can perhaps discuss why you feel this way and how to cope with it. Even if you haven't figured this one out yet for yourself, chat with your child about it. Don't pretend that you have it all figured out. You may be surprised how these open discussions can strengthen ties with your surviving children. In many ways this may help you with your own healing process. You are building on existing bonds with your other children.

You will notice that no two surviving siblings grieve the same way. Once again proof that all grief is unique and very personal. Let each of your children discuss their fears either in private, or encourage an open family discussion where everyone can share. Sometimes this can not only allow your child to free themselves of the emotions that have been haunting them since their sibling's death. It may allow other siblings to confirm whether they are feeling the same way. When there are common emotions it becomes easier to work through each of your children's fears.

Some of the fears and emotions your children may be feeling are very real. They may become paranoid that something similar is going to happen to another member of your immediate family unit. This is rather tricky because you cannot make this promise. You don't have a crystal ball or ultimate control over the natural order of things in the universe. What you can guarantee your child is that there will always be a support structure in place that they can rely on. Let them know who this circle of people will be. Include yourself and your spouse. If you have another external extended family that will be around for them.

Some of your children may still be quite small. At the time of the loss of their sibling, don't bombard them with words they cannot understand, or all at once. Break things down into words they can understand. Check in with them as you explain things to them whether they understand. Do they have any questions? They may need a couple of days to process what you have told them. This doesn't mean they haven't understood you, it just means they are trying to figure it out in their own minds.

It is these smaller children that you might want to get involved in planting a tree, building a commemorative rock garden, and drawing a picture to commemorate their sibling.

Children this age are going to need a lot of nurturing to help them heal. Keep a close eye on them to be sure that you are tending to each need as it arises. These emotions, questions, fears, questions, phobias, nightmares, and all sorts of other challenges are going to be experienced by your child. Maybe not all of them, but be prepared to deal with these and at your child's level, not your own. You may need to make contact with your therapist for some guidance on how to work with your child of this age, and maybe even other children of other ages. Grief doesn't hit children any less than adults. The loss of a loved one whether a child or a sibling is still a loss.

Other things that might be lost are deep connections. The closeness in relationships. These could be any relationships and for any number of reasons. Examples of this might include obvious relationships with married couples, relationships with parents and children where children play up simply in an attempt to get some form of recognition from parents who have buried themselves so far in their grief they have forgotten they have other children needing their attention.

Friendships. This is where cutting yourself off from those around you, possibly because they also have small children and it hurts too much to be with them can hurt your relationship as well. This is where your support is going to come from. Don't for one moment think that your friends' are not going to feel the loss of your friendship. They want to be there for you, and you have cut them off.

HEALING WHAT'S BROKEN WITHIN

There are two trains of thought when it comes to this topic.

The first is that you can be completely selfish, focusing on yourself. This is where you also keep your own emotions closely guarded. Effectively, you shut off to those around you. Chances are you are battling internally to come to terms with the immense loss you are feeling. All you know is that you are hurting. Whether you have the capacity or not, you simply cannot see that those around you are also having a hard time. That they may desperately need your help, your understanding, and sometimes just a sounding board or someone to cry with.

The second is to pretend that everything is okay. That you are strong enough to take on everyone in the family's pain, emotions, tears, fears, and grief of every description of yourself. During this process you are masking your own grief by trying to be of service to other members of the family.

There's one thing in being there to help and support other family members but you need to accept that part of the grieving process for everyone, including yourself is being able to feel and openly express your emotions to someone. It doesn't necessarily mean you need to redirect this to your family, especially if you want them to continue thinking that you have it all together but you do need help.

Find someone you can confide in long-term. This is not going to be a short journey, especially if you want to be strong enough for everyone.

Think about it for a second, you have essentially set yourself up to support the entire family, or majority of the family through everything they will be feeling about losing their child, and sibling.

Some ideas to help you along with this process is to encourage unity within the family unit. Getting back to previous sections, talk about your loved one. Something many families battle with is calling the child you have lost by their name. Whether this is out of reverence to the child or fear that a flood of emotions will overcome you if you have to give them space by mentioning their name. Fix this. If this is a challenge in your home, talk about it. Call them by their name and discuss all those happy memories each of you have with your child or their sibling. You may find that some of these memories you as a parent had no knowledge of. These are usually the memories that lighten the hollow emotions each family member is experiencing.

Have each family member choose to do something to honor the family member that has died.

Repair relationships that have been negatively affected. This may take admitting to fault and error on your part. It is worth admitting you are wrong for the sake of fixing these relationships whether they be with family or close friends.

WHAT GOES THROUGH YOUR MIND?

You may be in a situation where the child that died was your only child. This is perhaps the worst kind of pain parents can go through. There's no such thing as being able to focus on other children to help respect and honor their siblings. For parents it is just this massive devastating loss. There is nothing to replace it. You need time to process your grief. Sometimes this means being alone. And, we know what this leads to.

For those parents that stick together, it isn't going to be easy. The journey is sometimes long and has lots of pitfalls. This can be especially difficult when it is an infant death. These are times when too many questions are raised. Was there something more that could have been done to prevent it? Was there something they may have done to cause it? There are questions for God. These questions can turn to anger at God for the perception that He is punishing them and they don't know why.

All around you notice parents with healthy babies or children. Each time you see this, or happen to be in the company with these parents your heart breaks a little more. You question why your child had to die, and there are so many other children who are healthy, happy, and part of a family unit.

Those around you have no idea of what you are going through mentally. They don't understand why you pull away from social engagements, or even associate yourself with them. This is something really heartbreaking to go through. You have not only lost your child, but you are sacrificing friendships at the same time. Friendships that may have offered support during the time you need them most.

Why an infant's death is so hard is that there are so many things you are mourning. There will never be the thrill of watching them take their first steps, all those firsts. First words, first days at kindergarten, first reports... Pre-school, school, prom. In some instances it may be recitals, football games, little league, and so on. Even parents with older children would be able to identify with losing out on some of these experiences. Walking a radiant daughter down the aisle, or standing tall and proud alongside your son and his wife as the next generation is born and the mantle of grandparent is placed on your shoulders as protector of another beautiful baby. You know, and mourn these future events that seem to be so cruelly stolen from you.

This is a pain that all parents losing a child will experience, not just those mourning the loss of an infant. You and your spouse go through the greatest shock and trauma to be experienced emotionally by any individual. You may feel you want another child as quickly as possible. Not to replace the child you have lost, because if anything you should realize that this can happen. Even if you manage to get this right, be prepared for your emotions toward your new child to be completely different.

There may be an array of reasons preventing you from having another child immediately. The most common of these is that your physical body has experienced such a massive trauma that everything is out of whack. If you are the mother. The devastation of having to go through the death of your child can affect your hormones, other physical organs, even within your brain which controls every part of you. This discussion needs to come from your medical professional so your husband understands what's going on internally. This may be the greatest challenge you go through as a couple. Not being able to have another child for a while.

Your fix in this instance is understanding one another, being able to discuss how you are really feeling, even if that is anger or frustration toward your spouse. Talk through each of these emotions to reach that point of understanding. It may mean that one of you needs to give in for the sake of the other. If you reach this point as a couple, you, and your marriage stands an excellent chance of being able to survive the loss of your baby.

Being able to work through the plethora of emotions you will begin to understand what those around you are going through. You will also learn how to become a better person especially toward your spouse.

FEELINGS FROM YOUR HEART

This is really being emotionally aware. It is normal to feel as if your heart is completely shattered into a million pieces. You cannot accept that there can be anything to repair it. This hollowness left in a heart aching so badly there are days when it feels like the shards from your broken heart have the capacity to stab you further and deeper it all becomes too much. Times like these require extreme support whether from your spouse or your trusted support group.

The only way to begin to work through emotions weighing heavily on your heart is making the decision that you are in so much pain that you need some form of assistance, whether this reaching out for some kind of intervention. There's a strong possibility that you have no clue what this intervention should look like. All the time you need to keep in the back of your mind that what you are experiencing right now is the greatest trial you will experience in your life.

Don't feel you need to apologize to anyone because you are feeling heartbroken, and you are feeling helpless. You feel like your life is over. And in some way, this is true. The life you had before is no longer there. What you knew as "normal," is now lying in pieces at your feet. There's nothing wrong with feeling lost and possibly in a daze. Even if this lasts for an extended period. Getting over a broken heart is impossible. The only thing you can do is work through each of your emotions and feelings you are experiencing. Don't expect to be able to work through each of these. This is impossible. There will always be emotions that are very unique to you that you may carry with you for the rest of your life. There's no point in trying to sugarcoat this for you. It simply isn't possible.

WHAT IS YOUR HEAD TELLING YOU?

You are always told that there is a difference between head and heart. This is no different when you try and work through the death of your child. Your mind is what does its best to make logical sense of what you are going through. Stop and think about this for a moment. Where do feelings and emotions come from? Those are predominantly physical. So, where does this leave your mind?

Your mind is responsible for all those questions, and thoughts that plague you. Even if you believe you have a grip on things mentally, all of a sudden there's some new memory that pops into your mind. Your mind may be questioning your parenting skills. It will question each emotional thought you have had since the devastating final news was delivered. From that moment your heart or head may have been in control. Each would have their turn because that is the natural order of life. You wouldn't be human if you didn't have thoughts to process. Emotions can physically be felt, whereas, thoughts can transport you all over the place.

There is extreme danger in working through our thoughts. These come with those thoughts of guilt, and thoughts that life is no longer worth living. When losing a child I believe that these two thoughts are experienced by everyone. Thoughts that through "checking out" you no longer have to work through all the things running around your brain. This is known as ruminating. Would you believe that the mind thinks of about 40,000 things daily. These cross your mind and your brain has a way of processing them to help you focus on those that are most important. When you feel your thoughts racing, this is exactly what is happening. You are no different from any other parent who has lost a child.

The only difference is that these thoughts are yours and once again are completely unique to you. What is important about thinking, and maybe overthinking can potentially lead to mental health problems. Don't get me wrong, I am no medical, or mental health practitioner, however, I can tell you that it doesn't happen to everyone. It is worth consulting with your GP or therapist to gauge where your thoughts are. This would be in a combined state with your emotions—if the one is strong while the other is lacking, these can balance one another out.

Please don't view each of these thoughts as leading to a life of doom and gloom, instead, be realistic that they are there. If your thinking goes this route, don't be afraid to ask for help before you do end up having to work through other ways to deal with your trauma,

HOW MANY OF THESE THINGS CAN BE FIXED?

In all honesty this is up to each individual. Many of their heartache, and emotional pain can be healed to some degree. Something to remember is that although possible it is going to take constant effort. Whether this is effort on behalf of the parents and other family members, or ongoing effort of those within a dedicated support group.

I have mentioned that your initial support system has very often moved on only to find another cause to help. I also mentioned that there will be those who will be with you throughout your process, even if it means sticking with you to the end. I know of parents who have just such a dedicated friend who has been there for them constantly and it is heading to four decades since they lost their baby. She will make calls, send messages, and connect every so often. I can only wish for a close friend like this for each of you. The sheer dedication of being there constantly and consistently is the key to genuine support.

You can possibly fix some of your emotions. That's not to say you will be able to keep them completely checked permanently. There will always be something to trigger your emotions. Dates on the calendar. What about all special occasions? Birthdays, commemorating the day of their death. Visiting their grave or spending time on a park bench if you have scattered their ashes. That quietness where you can be alone with your thoughts will bring you back to the point where you are still trying to make some kind of sense of it all.

Anyone that tells you "things get better with time" has never lost a child. They may have lost a loved one, which brings with it another completely different set of emotions… These are nowhere near anything a parent or sibling will experience. If individuals who are prone to using this overused phrase as a means of comforting a parent or siblings experiencing such a devastating loss, get over yourselves. You have no idea what you are talking about! There are parents who continue to mourn their child decades later. They always will. These parents don't go throughout a single day without thinking about the child they never got to raise.

These parents are not going to wear the story of their loss on their sleeves. It will be something extremely personal, and possibly even sacred to them. Even when they do have other children, they will explain to them that they had an older brother or sister. This will in turn involve the entire family unit. Parents should be aware of making this news positive rather than negative and somber. Naturally, this will only be discussed with your children as they are old enough to understand what the difference between life and death is.

An ideal time may be if they experience the death of another loved member of the family, possibly in the form of a grandparent, aunt, or uncle. When there is a strong bond between them they can grasp the concept of what loss feels like. What they are going through can help you segue into explaining to them that they had another sibling who died. Don't harp on this discussion. You may have photographs in your home. This might also provide you with opportunities to discuss the real family dynamic.

Something to avoid is being overprotective of your next children. When you explain the loss of their sibling, they may suddenly gain a better understanding of why you have perhaps been overprotective. Once you explain your rationale to your child or other children, it may be time to loosen the reins a bit. You can do whatever you want, despite all the paranoia in the world, if accidents are going to happen they will happen. Unfortunately we cannot control the natural order of things. All we can do is accept and live our very best lives, celebrating the time with each child in turn. It also means becoming grateful for each season we have with each child, and especially the one that was taken far too early according to your thinking.

ACCEPTING WHEN SOME THINGS WILL ALWAYS BE

Some of this was touched on above. You do come to a point in your life where you have to accept that what transpired has to be. There is nothing you can do to change what has happened. No amount of self-berating, guilt, anger, frustration, hurt, devastation, blame, anxiety, doubt, and any other emotion you can add to the above can change the outcome. You cannot escape the experience or the pain you experienced.

Getting to this point of accepting the death of a child is not predictable. Nobody can put a time on it. There's no alarm clock to indicate that your time of mourning is now over and you need to return to normality. All you have to do is speak to any parent who has lost a child at any age.

They will each share their own journey to getting to that point, if they feel comfortable enough to do so. Don't expect every parent to tell you that they have accepted the death of their child, irrespective of the amount of time having elapsed. I have already mentioned that some parents never get to the point of full acceptance. The reason for saying this is because there will always be a part of them that feels the deep loss for the child that is no longer there.

One can hope that all parents can finally reach a point of acceptance and the peace that this knowledge, or belief might bring with the decision. Once again, this decision of acceptance does not mean having to cut ties with all the memories you will always hold dear, the photographs, the precious feelings you carry in your heart. There will be nothing to replace these, ever.

KEY TAKEAWAYS

- Losing your child will overwhelm you, your thoughts and emotions will become so overcome. Constant thoughts make it difficult to see the things that need urgent attention to be the strength and support to your spouse and other children. This is just one of the things that are broken because of the traumatic experience you are trying to overcome.

- Appreciate that you need to look at what is happening around you. What is happening within your children. How can you be of assistance to each of them? Do whatever you can to help them understand what is happening. Be sure your child is old enough to understand what you mean when you explain that they have a sibling that is no longer there. They need to understand life and death, and what this means to them. Allow them to decide whether to participate in any memorial rituals you may already have in place.

- Be prepared to have challenging experiences in both heart and head, although each is covered separately, these can also be at odds with one another, making these intensely broken bits of ourselves even more challenging to be able to work through.

- There is some form of healing that can come from getting to the point of "acceptance." Do what you need to do to reach this point. Those around you should understand there is no timetable to reaching this point. No alarm clock will awaken parents to move through the steps outlined in the Grief process.

- Unfortunately, there are some things that cannot be fixed. This is sometimes hard for parents to accept. Sometimes it can take years before you even reach a point where you can even talk about your loss let alone get to a point of discussing this with others. Don't be afraid of letting others in, and even asking others for help. There is no harm in doing whatever is necessary for you to move forward.

CHAPTER 7
EMBRACING SHARED SORROW: FINDING UNITY IN GRIEF

> "In a few weeks her partner will find the box containing the crib in the storeroom, the one she kept nagging at him to put together, and he'll sob so hard that it feels like his ribs will break. For the rest of their lives they will always walk past the display windows of the sport shop and think that there's one bicycle too many in there. A pair of skates too many. A hundred thousand adventures and trees to climb and puddles to jump in too many. A million uneaten ice creams. They will never be woken too early on holiday mornings, never whisper-shout "Quiet!" when they're talking on the phone, never put small gloves on the radiator. The greatest fear, the tiniest human, will never be theirs."
> **Frederik Backman (2022)**

This was shared with me by someone I met during my grief counseling support group. During the time I really needed them we became really close and while our stories were somewhat different we shared losing a child. While I have her permission to share her story here, I still wish to respect her anonymity. In doing so, let's refer to her as "Becky."

She and her husband enjoyed their first year of marriage blissfully in love. They had been and were still best friends. Before getting married they dated for seven years. By the end of their first year of marriage, Becky discovered she was pregnant! It was not a planned pregnancy. Neither felt they were near ready to be parents. They were still in the honeymoon stage of their lives. Becky especially felt she had so much living to still do.

Despite all their initial feelings these would soon turn to genuine excitement for the brand-new addition to their home. They were going to be a family! There was nothing out of the ordinary throughout her pregnancy and the doctors were all convinced everything would go just as planned. Becky was young and healthy. Her mind was in the right place, and they were more than ready for this monumental experience.

Becky went into labor about two weeks before her actual due date. She stuck through seventeen hours of labor but forgot all about the pain when she finally held her precious little girl. Any mother knows how no matter how much pain you had to experience through the birth of your child is completely forgotten once you count all those tiny fingers and toes.

This was exactly what happened to Becky and her husband Paul. Suddenly it seemed as though a natural nurturing intuition took over. Sure, they were given the basics of how to hold a baby correctly, feeding, changing, and bathing, all the time becoming more and more attached and in awe of a little creation that was a perfect result of the love they shared between them.

A month or so went by. Everything seemed to be perfect. All pediatric appointments were kept, their little girl was perfectly healthy in every way.

Suddenly she wasn't. There would be no indication, symptoms, or reason for what happened next.

Paul would sometimes work away from home several days each month. It just so happened he was away on this particular night. Becky went through her normal ritual of bathing, feeding and settling her daughter to sleep, placing her in her crib, ensuring the room temperature was right. She then went about cleaning, and sorting out their home, before turning in for the night herself.

Every parent, or mother at least learns to sleep lightly, often waking at the least little whimper. It was not unusual for her to sleep, waking at different times of the night to check up on her tiny daughter. On this particular night she would discover her little girl unresponsive and turning blue. She ran screaming to her closest neighbors, with this tiny baby's lifeless body in her arms. Her neighbors were quick to attempt CPR, Becky had been taught all of this but in her panicked state, all her training went out the window.

She couldn't even remember who was driving, but the other kept attempting CPR on this tiny body.

Arriving at the hospital's emergency room, she ran with her baby directly to a medical professional on duty. All the while screaming "My baby's dying, my baby's dying." She described how she had a million emotions swirling through her mind simultaneously. She sat in a frozen state while doctors kept working on her child. She reasoned within herself that she would be alright… she just had to be.

She described how she felt when the doctors returned to the waiting area with sullen faces. Becky's legs gave way under her, and she fell to the ice cold stone floor sobbing uncontrollably… Some form of masked reality would kick in. Perhaps it was a form of self-preservation. So she could function on the surface despite all the emotions she was really feeling beneath. She would compose herself enough to approach the doctors requesting to see her daughter before they took her away.

She was escorted to an emergency room cubicle. This beautiful little girl looked peaceful, despite having taken her last breath almost moments before Becky went to check on her. If she wasn't gray and icy it would be easy to mistake thinking she was simply in a deep sleep.

Why? What was the explanation for how a perfectly healthy baby girl could be snatched away without any signs of illness beforehand. The doctors would ask a string of questions. She couldn't understand this at the time. They were searching for answers themselves. Finally, they could explain to Becky what caused her daughter to be snatched from their family. She had never heard of their final prognosis before. The cause of death was listed as sudden infant death syndrome, or SIDS. Having seen her child after the doctors had done their best to revive her, she explains how a calm came over her and a feeling of acceptance. Was it being able to see her daughter, or having her public meltdown on the floor of the hospital, she now had enough strength to move forward.

Her phone calls to Paul and other extended family were gut-wrenching. Her mother gave her the most support and consolation. Paul was devastated. He held himself responsible. Why had he not been there? He may have picked up on it sooner. He left to return home immediately. There had to have been a mistake. She could not be dead, When he left a couple of days before, she was still jovial, gurgling at the funny faces he made at her. Her dark brown eyes glistened as she could recognize each of her parents.

Reading up more on SIDS, causes, statistics, and all information they could lay their hands They discovered an alarming amount of boxes they could tick when it came to their daughter's routine. The questions now became centered around all the WHY's.

Funeral arrangements were taken over by Becky's mom, and there would be a host of family, and friends to provide support.

Normally, an autopsy would be done by the medical examiner to determine cause of death. This could be declined by the family. Paul was adamant that this be denied. They would accept the cause of death as SIDS. There was nothing more they could do other than try to support each other through a very difficult time. Paul would go through a phase of blaming Becky for not paying attention, checking on her regularly, for not getting help sooner... Naturally, this would put massive dents in their what once seemed iron-clad relationship. This also left Becky questioning her actions that evening. Was Paul right?

The funeral came and went, Becky has recollections of dressing her daughter in one of her special white dresses. She was still so tiny at just over three months. Through it all, Becky held her own, and when people asked her how she was doing, she would answer that she was at peace with God's plan and was trying to figure it out for herself! She felt more vulnerable than ever before. She had not only failed as a mother, but was now failing Paul as a wife.

Becky remained calm and composed to everyone's shock. She explained that it was so bad that people began thinking she was heartless. That she never really cared for her child. There would even be whispers and malicious rumors that she may have even had a hand in her daughter's death. Becky couldn't wait for everyone to leave her alone. Others may have recognized that this was how she was, Becky was silently trying to process things, she would insist she was feeling okay about it. Although at the time she was far from okay.

The relationship with Becky and Paul became strained. He also believed for a while that there was something wrong with Becky. Why wasn't she feeling the same heartbreak as he was? Why didn't she express her emotions? Her behavior was completely out of character. Perhaps she needed to meet with a qualified mental health professional. All the constant insistence over her emotions and whether she did or didn't express them the way those around her wanted her to, made her appear to him as almost a freak of nature. How could any mother just switch off all her emotions?

The failure to speak freely, openly, and honestly drove a wide wedge between Becky and Paul. It wouldn't be long before their marriage was on the skids, each going their own way, despite the deep love they had for one another. Their own grieving process was completely misunderstood by the others. Instead of being supportive they were at constant odds with each other.

Despite the hurt, heartache and pain in finally parting, they realized they would never be able to be truly happy through the grieving process. This is just one example of how the death of a loved one can impact relationships to the extreme. Many times, resulting in the ultimate point of desperation, where you find the only way to survive yourself is by cutting your partner off completely.

It would take Becky almost a decade before the death of her daughter would finally hit her. She had a complete meltdown, and a psychiatric episode. Not pleasant, but her wounds were so deep, and pushed down so far that it would take seven years to finally reach the surface resulting in a massive explosion that for those who knew her long enough could finally understand that it wasn't that she didn't care about her child or was heartless. At the time of her loss she couldn't find a way to express her emotions and work through them.

Sadly, Paul and Becky divorced within a couple of years of losing their daughter. She often reminisces over the loss of her child, and her husband. You see, on that day, she not only lost the tiny piece of her heart but she lost the love of her life as well.

Today, Becky is the proud mother of four healthy children. She wasn't able to conceive for seven years. Does she still hurt? You bet! She will be the first one to tell you that whenever she sees someone who would more or less be the same age as her first daughter would have been, she is immediately transported right back to that moment. She wonders what her daughter would have been like? Would she have been a graduate? What would all her ambitions and aspirations have been? Would they have a strong relationship? Perhaps Becky may even have been a grandparent herself by then.

From the time she wakes up each morning, the first thoughts are directly associated with her daughter. Throughout the day she will have random memories or fleeting moments of these few days when she was alive. As evening falls, her last thoughts at night may often be of her child.

Her mind has been constantly wracked with all those "what if…" questions. Questions where she replays the situation over, and over through her head, each with different scenarios and possibly where the outcome may perhaps have been different. Part of the problem that led to the breakdown of her marriage to Paul was that she was living in her own little bubble. She never took into account how Paul might be thinking or feeling about the loss himself. She forgot that this child belonged to both of them. She was a combination of both of them.

Earlier I touched on when you first receive that final diagnosis that the prognosis and outlook for your child is the last thing you want to hear. You remember the first time they collapsed. That first doctor's visit, waiting for test results time and time again as more and more specialists became involved in the process. You fully understood what an oncologist did. No amount of prayers would hold back the ax that delivered the final blow. As if cancer wasn't bad enough, having something you could hardly pronounce should have given you an indication of how serious it was.

This was the experience of another close friend. Turns out the cancer diagnosed wasn't as foreign as she first thought it was just going to be rough on her young son. He would need to undergo extremely rigorous and aggressive treatment. He needed an urgent bone marrow transplant. While this sounded something like being put on a transplant list for an organ transplant, the reality was that finding a suitable donor, or a DNA match was much more difficult. It cost way more. Firstly, there was an upside. If a member of the family were a suitable match this meant now waiting to go on lists and so forth, your child could simply receive all the treatment to prepare them for the transplant, something extremely challenging, and physically taxing on its own. A familial match at least gives your child a chance.

The testing process is extremely painful. Having each member of the family go through the process was emotionally draining. It was making everyone aware of the severity of the severity of their child's illness. Next came the prayers and test of faith that amid all the samples at least one would be suitable.

It would take one look at the doctor's face to know the outcome of the tests without a word. Next would come full circle with a medical treatment plan for their son who was only getting weaker as each day passed. Donor sites, societies, and organizations would be notified globally in a hope and a prayer that there would be some suitable match somewhere. With each communication and test performed costs will escalate. This would be ignored this because no price was greater than the price of their son.

There would come a cut off point. A stage when their child became so weak from trying to fight off the cancer attacking his small body that he was depleted and it was physically apparent he had given all he could possibly give.

Every avenue had come up empty.

She said they would forever remember the call from their doctor telling them to come to the hospital with their family. This was the last hurdle for their child. Whether they knew it or not at the time, it would only just be the first hurdle for them as parents. Their immediate family would be there for their son. Siblings would say their tearful goodbyes. As parents they wouldn't be sure until much later whether the other children understood what was meant by that farewell.

As a couple, they would have some special time to hold and kiss little hands and foreheads. They could caress tousled curls or arms that had lost so much weight they were now skeletal. The doctor confirmed there was no longer any hope and it would be a matter of hours.

All they could do is pretend to be strong. Hold back the ocean of tears threatening to wash them away in that sea of emotions they just know would take them ages to come to terms with. They held their son's tiny hands in their without letting go long after the doctor has legally pronounced him dead. The word itself is one they had, and still have had nightmares over hearing ever since. They admit that they don't know when these nightmares will end.

LESSONS YOU MAY BE ABLE TO USE

This kind of death almost seems to have a slightly better chance at being able to survive as a family unit. Whether it is because it was always in the back of your minds as a partnership. Perhaps you had even discussed a coping strategy. Not that this strategy always works. You may find emotions running high throughout your home. When this happens it is perhaps better if the whole family gets involved.

This death touches everyone, not just you as parents. Even if children are removed from a room before their sibling dies. Don't insult your children's intelligence. They can feel a very similar loss.

In a lot of instances these same children will do everything in their power to try and keep things together for the sake of their parents and younger siblings. When we are crushed the incorrectly assume that this role and responsibility is theirs to carry. No child should be expected to live up to these expectations.

TRYING TO SURVIVE AS A SINGLE PARENT

How does a single parent work through the death of a child without someone to lean on? The one thing about being part of a large grief support group is that you get to hear stories shared by others that share the one thing in common. The death of a child and doing their best to work through the grief process. The following is a story shared with the permission of one of the member's in my group.

Let's call her Emma. She had been widowed for a number of years, left with four children spaced just a year apart. Her children were part of a group that would spend time practicing little league during each week. Because Emma was the sole breadwinner she was forced to work and had to rely on another mother to transport her sons to practice and home each week. Because she knew the other so well she trusted her with her three sons. Her daughter would go with to cheer her brothers along.

She recalls that the call she received was the most spine chilling news ever. Possibly even more so than losing her husband.

Headed home after practice another light passenger vehicle had hit them head on while attempting to overtake a slower moving vehicle. The car was hit with such force that it rolled before coming to rest against guardrails and brushing several hundred meters away. It seemed miraculous that anyone within the SUV had survived. Everyone would emerge with a couple of bumps and scratches. Everyone except her youngest son that is!

He had not been sitting in a spot that would cause him to be in any more danger than his siblings or friends. It just turned out that he would die instantly. The police and other investigators weren't able to provide Emma with any further clarity on why it was that she had lost her one child while the other three had walked away with minor injuries. What would manifest further down the line was that the siblings that survived had to find their own coping mechanisms. That and their own ways to commemorate the loss of their brother.

Today, while most of these children are parents themselves, they still remember the brother they lost and are possibly more grateful for life because of it.

The three surviving siblings would need to take the place of their father in being supportive of their mother. All the while Emma would do her best not to show her children how desperately sad she was, and how she was experiencing that overloaded loss we discussed earlier, the one thing she had was the love, support, and understanding of her other three children because they were present. They knew how miraculous it was that they got to walk away.

The lesson for each of them was to be grateful for being alive each new day.

This memory holds very special memories for each surviving family member. No matter how long ago his death took place. Even when decades go by, the pain is never gone. Be grateful each time someone is willing to open up and be vulnerable enough to share some of the most devastating times of their lives.

Reliving any of these experiences is painful for each survivor. In most instances the reason for them sharing their story is to help you work through your own pain or grief. Listen to the ways they manage their own grief. No one is forcing you to follow any of these recommendations but there just may be something they did that can offer you a glimmer of hope in dealing with the pain you are currently experiencing.

CHAPTER 8
SPOTTING RAINBOWS: SEEKING RAYS OF LIGHT AMIDST GRIEF

> "Grief, I've learned, is really just love. It's all the love you want to give, but cannot. All that unspent love gathers up in the corners of your eyes, the lump in your throat, and in that hollow part of your chest. Grief is just love with no place to go."
> **Jamie Anderson (Luc, 2021)**

Throughout the chapters above there have been stories of loss. Stories of grief that are very real. There's no one that can take that away from you, and in the words of Elisabeth Kübler-Ross,

> The reality is that you will grieve forever. You will not 'get over' the loss of a loved one; you will not learn to live with it. You will heal and you will rebuild yourself around the loss you have suffered. You will be whole again but you will never be the same. Nor should you be the same nor would you want to (Kübler-Ross & Byock, 1969/2014).

The advice given above is timeless, for all parents or all ages, and in all situations. She may have developed that five step grieving process that you may have bounced around in and out a couple of times before getting to this point. A point of acceptance and peace, or at least searching for peace.

There comes a time after losing something as precious as a child where you have beaten yourself up enough, you have blamed, hated, been angry with those around you, angry at God for taking a child that belonged to you. That time comes whether you become exhausted at fighting through each day that you give in and just let the process flow.

Believe it or not, it takes so much effort and energy being angry. It is exhausting. Once you realize this, you will also recognize how many other things you have sacrificed. You may have missed key moments in the lives of your surviving children. How sad for both of you. Hopefully through reading this you gain some clarity that grief is necessary. It is okay for you to work through everything you need to for you to try and reach that point of "Acceptance" that much quicker. It needs to be genuine acceptance though so you can move onto this next phase of your life.

Leaving all the gut wrenching feelings of sadness and loss so deep that heartbreak and feeling as though your entire body physically experienced a piece within you die alongside your child.

The space you want to move into now is looking for those rainbows. It is easy to see the dark clouds building as a storm or downfall is about to happen. Because you know the storm is about to erupt or rage you get to prepare for it. You pack your umbrella and suitable shoes to see yourself through the downfall.

As the sky clears, the clouds turn white, dissipating revealing a clear blue sky.

We seldom survey our surroundings. All you need to do is look around you. Chances are you will find multiple rainbows one above the other each arching way above the other. Whether you practice faith and believe in God, you will again see His hand and realize that He is in control. He has got you no matter where you are on your path of grief. That rainbow is a promise. One where there are better days to come. That there is hope to be found amid your loss.

Perhaps you believe in other Higher interventions, whether it be the Universe or other form of deity, the message is the same. The archway of multiple bright colors, whether argued that it is simply caused due to light refracting from the earth. Choose to believe whatever you want but there are better days ahead.

Choose to associate with those that are positive in their outlook. In an ever changing world that has been hit with so many difficult challenges, it can be simple to decide to curl into a ball too afraid to interact with anyone. You may simply find people physically, mentally, and emotionally draining. Don't give in or allow them to influence your healing. It is easy to be derailed especially when you are going through that sensitive transitional phase as you reach "Acceptance" and peace.

There is hope to be found amid your loss that seems to have brought nothing but chaos and disorder to your life. Some of the ways to discover this hope is to accept that:

Grief never ends.

It will always be there.

The only thing that changes is the severity of the grief you are experiencing and how it manifests itself. You may be wondering what I mean when I say that grief can manifest itself in different ways. It has the potential to swallow you whole. You know this because you have already experienced it. Having reached this point, you should recognize the signs and know how to get around this manifestation. It can manifest itself with memories of darker times. Times where you were uncertain whether you wanted to keep going or not. Times where you were pulled through by people that loved you, your faith, your will to live for other members of your family, this list can go on. The point is you were pulled through. Where you really want to be is where your manifestation is going to bring you to this point where all you remember and replay within you are those memories that make you laugh and smile. Those tender moments. The mischievous moments. Perhaps you are fortunate enough to have captured some of these moments digitally. You will find peace and comfort going through these fun, positive memories of someone that was loved so very deeply.

There is a connection between recovery versus integration. You don't recover from the loss yet it is something that gets integrated in your life—and hopefully turns you into a better and more resilient person.

Finding hope means working at keeping their memory alive. It possibly means forcing yourself initially to search through all the negativity and sadness to cut through the hurt. This may mean shedding those tears. Just like the storm, to get to those smiles and memories that will bring you happiness, you will need to make a concerted effort.

I know of parents who lost children three- and four decades ago. They will tell you their pain is the same. The way they think about their child is different. I am not even going to promise a magic wand or potion to take it away.

For some it means chatting with a photograph of their child each day, and no, there's nothing freaky about this… Unless their child answered of course. This can offer that reassurance of keeping their child alive by actually doing something.

I can guarantee there are parents who wake up first thing in the morning with thoughts turning to the child they lost. You are not going nuts, you have found a coping mechanism that works for you. This is your rainbow.

Some may devote their thoughts at night time to their child. While this seems to still be a noble way of keeping your child in your thoughts the only caveat is that due to the time of day you may drift off to sleep with these thoughts. If they are in the least bit negative or depressing you might find yourself experiencing nightmares or being unsettled.

What rainbow are you looking for?

This is what you, and only you can answer. As a parent, you get the front-row seat to the way your life is playing out. The way I see it, by the time you reach acceptance for the final time (this means you are no longer bouncing between the stages of grief like a pinball machine on overdrive) you reach a crossroad. You get to choose which way you go. Do you look for that rainbow where the sky is the most brilliant, azure blue without a cloud in sight? The sun is out, and you know the rainbow will soon be gone.

With it, all the emotions you have experienced to this point. Your choice is to replace it all with happiness.

The second, in the opposite direction, still has a rainbow, however the storm clouds are still there. The sun is not quite out. If you reach this point, you might want to turn on your heels and run like hell in the other direction.

Even remembering your child each day can be done out of pure love. You can experience happiness again. You will laugh again, you will experience pure joy… And peace. That peace you may have been searching for all along.

KEY TAKEAWAYS

- Accept grief forever. The intensity differs.

- Look for each rainbow after the most turbulent of storms. Whether you see bright sunlight or merely a slight clearing, the rainbow will be there and with it, the promise of peace.

- Choose how you will honor and remember your child.

- You can be happy again and you deserve to find peace. Allow yourself to find it again.

CONCLUSION
WHISPERS OF HEALING: EMBRACING LOVE, JOY, AND BEAUTY AMIDST GRIEF"

> *"It is the capacity to feel consuming grief and pain and despair that also allows me to embrace love and joy and beauty with my whole heart, I must let it all in."*
> **Anna White (Levins, 2020)**

The sad part of losing a child for any parent is that unfortunately, there are some things which cannot be fixed. Parents may find this hard to accept. This isn't just an initial acceptance. They may never get over it. Talking about their loss may be too traumatic for them to even consider doing for years. If something can be learned from everything contained in this book, it is that you should not be too afraid to let others in. It's okay to ask for help. There are people in the form of your very own support group standing by to help you.

Of course, you don't need to do any of these things. If you feel you can't move forward just yet, that's also okay, so long as you don't paralyze yourself in this state. If you are within a complete family unit think about how your decisions and actions will affect those who are around you and may even be relying on you. By a complete family unit I am referring to a committed couple with either the child they have just lost, or other children.

It can be selfish of a parent to go into hibernation or simply shutting themselves off from their spouse and the rest of their family. This is certainly going to place undue pressure on relationships. Not all of these are strong enough to withstand the pressure of what could well be accepted as complete absence from the needs of their family. This makes no difference which parent is choosing this route.

Losing a child cannot be compared with any other loss. Not even the loss of a parent or spouse is anywhere near. This is the most painful thing you will ever go through in your entire life. It is unrealistic to expect yourself, your spouse or children to pick up the pieces within a fixed time frame and get along with your lives. Grief, and grieving your child cannot be measured by time.

We may have mentioned the five stages of grief in Chapter 4. At the same time, we mentioned that these steps are fluid, meaning there is no pattern to which step comes first, second, and so on. It also means that until you are genuinely at the point of final acceptance you will continue visiting different stages of grief. Although there are five stages in the grieving process, you don't necessarily have to work through all of them. Some of them may be well within your control, it is the others you need to beware of.

A grieving parent can mask their true emotions and even anxieties behind what appears to be a well-organized and put-together parent. If you are on the other side of this relationship, look for tiny cracks. If your partner seems to be handling things too well, it may be time to take a time out to have a frank and genuine heart-to-heart open communication. Possibly one of the most important lessons to be learned is that communication all around is vital for healing.

Whether this means being able to communicate with each other as partners, and communicating with other family members in the form of other children. Establish ground rules for communication, especially between parents and surviving children. The worst thing would be losing another child along the way… Not physically, but mentally, and emotionally because they never felt heard.

It is possible that if communication is established between parents that are going through the most excruciating pain will recognize what the other needs or is lacking. Remember that this is not always possible. There will be that parent that pulls away or withdraws completely. They insist they are okay, regardless of who is asking. This may be years and even decades before this all comes tumbling down. It may be seen as delayed grief. The unfortunate thing about experiencing delayed grief is that the original support system is no longer there. It is seldom that anyone within the current circle is even aware that there is a history of losing a child.

Times like these need intervention. Whether it is group therapy with a grief counseling group similar to Alcoholics Anonymous, a therapist specializing in grief counseling, a family therapist, a psychologist or if serious enough, a psychiatrist. Wherever this fracture leads, appropriate intervention needs to happen. With a bit of luck you haven't blown up your marriage and it may be time for your spouse to finally be able to step out from behind the shadows of your brave front. You may finally allow them in to help you. Allowing them to see you experiencing those vulnerable and raw emotions. The demons they were forced to slay on their own. Because of this, they are the only ones who really understand exactly what you are going through.

Do the work. Becoming a survivor in the family unit means working through all sorts of emotions that will take you all over the place and can hit you from any direction at any time. The question is how well prepared you are to be strong enough to work through these feelings.

Even talking about your child that died is painful. This needs to be one of the top priorities because anything less than this begins to dehumanize them like you are trying to erase them from your home, your family, and your environment. This is impossible to do. There will be sometime when this will all come to a head. If this is something you are doing at the moment then ask for help.

When working through your emotions and coping with the death of your child, some of the emotions will include guilt, self-blame, and even self-pity. Something to take into serious consideration is that we don't choose what enters into our minds and we should never shut these emotions out. They are there with a purpose and are trying to tell us something. We need to validate them, listen, and respect them and only then reassure them that they don't need to take control.

Shutting all these emotions out will only help them manifest in silence and spill over into other areas of your life. Don't ignore when these feeling happen. Don't be too hard on yourself. You already know emotions will occur. Of course, you have no control of when or where this can happen. Something to remember as you work through all these emotions is that nothing will change the fact that no amount of mourning will ever bring your child back. Take as long as you need to be able to accept this.

Something that may happen, and you need to know that it is not new, it is for you and possibly both you and your spouse to feel guilty, useless as parents, and question your ability to take care of your surviving children. If you are choosing to believe that you are unworthy of your children and that God is somehow punishing you, this is all part of the process within the steps of grief. There is nothing you can do to bring your child back again.

Accept that you all grieve differently. There is a difference between the way one spouse grieves to that of the other. You may be best friends but see your experience completely differently. Don't try and force your partner to think differently or convince them that they cannot be experiencing things that you are. In truth they may not be going through what you are. Instead, they may be facing something a lot worse that you still need to deal with further down the line.

Working through grief is like being on a rollercoaster. The difference being that each member of the family is located at a different point, and sometimes on a completely different track. There will be some place where they will all intersect.

It may take a lot of time and patience to get there. Patience, understanding, and something that hasn't been mentioned till this point… Compassion. This gift is often seen as something you would offer a loved one in your family. Often the greatest gift of compassion is when you use it for yourself. This is where you give yourself permission to mourn without holding back, without a time-limit, without someone passing judgment because you are supposed to be this rough and ready, stoic male, or put-together mother who always seems to fix everything, always.

Remember that this is a first for everyone in your immediate family. Everyone grieves completely differently. There is a distinct difference between the way children will mourn their sibling to the way parents mourn the loss of their child. This pain is something that cannot be described or imagined. Only if you have walked or tried to walk this path that you get an idea of what you are going through. Why I mention "trying to," is because it is a process. There will always be something you will face out of nowhere that you need to spend some time working on.

The loss you try and process is so different that there may be times when you aren't even sure whether your partner is feeling anything whatsoever. This is probably one of the greatest misconceptions and reasons that lead to separation and divorce, especially at times like this when families should be sharing tender moments rather than casting judgment.

The thing is that how one member is working through their grief and displaying it is completely different from the other. Accept that everyone is hurting, On their own terms. At times we may need to take a few steps back to see what the big picture looks like from the outside.

This is where external interventions are helpful. If you find you can't cope with the rush of emotions, trying to make sense of them all, or simply recognize you can't do it alone anymore. There's no shame in asking for help. This is for all family members. Rely on your own support system surrounding you but recognize that there is only so much they can do. You may need professional help. If this is necessary, don't be afraid to go this route. Your main aim is to find the best way to work through the grief you are experiencing as a result of your loss.

If nothing else, rest assured that no matter the pain of your grieving process, how long it takes for you to get there, you will someday feel that sunlight of hope shining on your face once more. You will find hope and the peace you have possibly been searching for since the death of your child.

Hope springs eternal. Those rainbows are within reach.

"EXTENDING GRATITUDE: A HEARTFELT THANK YOU"

I want to express my heartfelt gratitude for entrusting me with your journey. Your trust is the foundation upon which this book was built. I sincerely hope that the words within these pages have provided a source of solace and guidance on your path to healing from grief. I understand the challenges you face, and I believe that, with time and dedication, healing is attainable. While the pain of separation lingers, may you find the strength to release the burden of carrying on without your loved one, allowing their memory to reside eternally in your heart and soul.

As I reflect on my dream and purpose, I envision reaching countless individuals around the world who are navigating the tumultuous waters of grief. If you find that this book has been a companion in your healing journey, I humbly ask for your support in sharing its message. By passing along this book, you have the power to extend a lifeline to someone else in need.

In the spirit of solidarity, I kindly request a small favor. If you have discovered value and comfort within these pages, I invite you to share your thoughts through a review on Amazon. Your words have the potential to guide future readers, offering them a glimpse into the transformative experience that awaits them.

Once again, thank you for embarking on this journey with me. May your path to healing be marked by moments of grace and the gradual mending of your heart.

With heartfelt appreciation,
Sheila West

OTHER TITLES YOU MIGHT LIKE, FROM SHEILA WEST.

THE MOST TRUSTED GUIDE TO HEALING AND RECOVERY

LIFE AFTER LOSS

HOW TO DEAL WITH GRIEF AND BEREAVEMENT AFTER THE DEATH OF A PARENT SPOUSE CHILD OR A LOVED ONE.

SHEILA WEST

DEAREST READERS
GET YOUR FREE GIFT!

REFERENCES
SOURCES OF INSIGHT: GUIDING LIGHT ON YOUR GRIEF JOURNEY

Backman, F. (2022). *The Winners*. Simon and Schuster.

Boland, M. (2021, July 22). *Quotes About Grief* (C. Cassata, Ed.). Psych Central. https://psychcentral.com/addictions/quotes-about-grief

Cancer.net Editorial Board. (2019, September). *Grieving the Loss of a Child*. Cancer.net. https://www.cancer.net/coping-with-cancer/managing-emotions/grief-and-loss/grieving-loss-child

Casabianca, S. (2021, February 11). *Mourning and the 5 Stages of Grief* (C. C. Cassell, Ed.). Psych Central. https://psychcentral.com/lib/the-5-stages-of-loss-and-grief

Chapple, R. (2023, February 21). *How to Deal With Grieving the Loss of a Child* (E. Keohan, Ed.). Talkspace. https://www.talkspace.com/blog/losing-a-child/

Choosing therapy. (2022 28). *Grieving the Loss of a Child: Coping & Moving Forward*. Choosing Therapy. https://www.choosingtherapy.com/loss-of-a-child/

Clarke, J. (2021, February 12). *How the Five Stages of Grief Can Help Process a Loss* (A. Morin, Ed.). Verywell Mind. https://www.verywellmind.com/five-stages-of-grief-4175361

Doka, K. J., & Martin, T. L. (2011). *Grieving Beyond Gender*. Routledge.

Duncan, J. R., & Byard, R. W. (2018, May). *Sudden Infant Death Syndrome: An Overview*. Nih.gov; University of Adelaide Press. https://www.ncbi.nlm.nih.gov/books/NBK513399/

Field, M. J., & Behrman, R. E. (2012). *Bereavement Experiences After the Death of Your Child*. Nih.gov; National Academies Press (US). https://www.ncbi.nlm.nih.gov/books/NBK220798/

Gerten, K. (2021, May 5). *It Hurts. 11 Quotes on Grief & Loss*. Youth Dynamics | Mental Health Care for Montana Kids. https://www.youthdynamics.org/it-hurts-11-quotes-on-grief-loss/

GoodReads. (n.d.). *A quote by Washington Irving*. Www.goodreads.com. https://www.goodreads.com/quotes/44057-there-is-a-sacredness-in-tears-they-are-not-a

Gupta, S. (2022, June 9). *What to Know About the Bargaining Stage of Grief* (Y. Renteria, Ed.). Verywell Mind. https://www.verywellmind.com/the-bargaining-stage-of-grief-characteristics-and-coping-5272529

Hayward, S. (2016, October 28). *How to talk to a parent who is in grief. From someone who's been there*. Mamamia. https://www.mamamia.com.au/ten-points-i-wish-every-person-knew-about-the-death-of-a-child/

Healgrief.org. (2019). *Grieving the Death of a Child*. HealGrief. https://healgrief.org/grieving-the-death-of-a-child/

Holland, K. (2023, May 17). *The Stages of Grief and What to Expect* (L. Lawrenz, Ed.). Healthline. https://www.healthline.com/health/stages-of-grief

James Henry, A. (2020, March). *The 8 Best Ways to Help Someone Who Has Lost a Child*. The Grief Recovery Method. https://www.griefrecoverymethod.com/blog/2020/03/8-best-ways-help-someone-who-has-lost-child

Kelly, L. (2021, September 23). *16 Different Types of Grief People Experience* (A. Ertel, Ed.). Talkspace. https://www.talkspace.com/blog/types-of-grief/

Knipfer, J. (2021). *In a Grove of Maples*. Jenny Knipfer--Author.

Kubala, K. (2022, July 27). *Top 10 Stressors That Can Trigger Anxiety* (S. Ferguson, Ed.). Psych Central. https://www.psychcentral.com/stress/top-10-life-stressors-that-can-trigger-anxiety

Kubler-Ross, E. (2014). *On grief and grieving* (2nd ed.). New York Scribner's. (Original work published 2005)

Kübler-Ross, E., & Byock, I. (2014). *On death & dying : what the dying have to teach doctors, nurses, clergy & their own families*. Scribner, A Division Of Simon & Schuster, Inc. (Original work published 1969)

Lee, J. (2020, September 11). *Activities to help with grieving for adults and children*. Peacefully. https://guide.peacefully.com/resources/activities-to-help-with-grieving-for-adults-and-children

Levins, M. L. B. (2020, December 18). *Words of Encouragement for Parents Who Lost a Child - Quotes*. Quotabulary. https://quotabulary.com/words-of-encouragement-for-parents-who-lost-a-child

Luc, H. (2021, May 6). *40 Comforting Quotes To Help You Heal After The Loss Of A Child*. YourTango. https://www.yourtango.com/quotes/losing-child-quotes-grieving-parents

Lyness, D. (2021, September). *When a Loved One Dies: How to help your child*. Kidshealth.org. https://kidshealth.org/en/parents/death.html

March of Dimes. (2017, October). *Dealing with grief after the death of your baby.* Www.marchofdimes.org. https://www.marchofdimes.org/find-support/topics/miscarriage-loss-grief/dealing-grief-after-death-your-baby

Miller, A. (2020, September 8). *Broken Heart Syndrome.* A Bed for My Heart. https://abedformyheart.com/broken-heart-syndrome/

Miller, A. (2021, July 21). *7 Things I Have Learned Since the Loss of My Child.* Compassionate Friends. https://www.compassionatefriends.org/blog/7-things-learned-since-loss-child/

Milne, B. (2022, August 4). *7 common types of grief (with examples).* Www.betterplaceforests.com. https://www.betterplaceforests.com/blog/articles/7-common-types-of-grief-with-examples

Mind Tools Content Team. (2023). *The Holmes and Rahe Stress Scale.* Www.mindtools.com. https://www.mindtools.com/avn893g/the-holmes-and-rahe-stress-scale

Morrow, A. (2023, February 16). *Finding the Right Words to Say When Someone Has Lost a Child* (I. O. Opole & J. Lacy, Eds.). Verywell Health. https://www.verywellfamily.com/what-do-i-say-to-a-grieving-parent-1132551

Reynolds, F. (2022, August 25). It has been 40 years since the death of our son. Grief is love that never leaves. *The Guardian.* https://www.theguardian.com/lifeandstyle/2022/aug/19/it-has-been-40-years-since-the-death-of-our-son-grief-is-love-that-never-leaves

Smith, C. (2020, October 12). *The Loss Of A Child Affects Parents Forever.* Scary Mommy. https://www.scarymommy.com/loss-of-child-affects-parents-forever

Snyder, M. V. (2014). *Storm glass.* Harlequin Mira. (Original work published 2013)

Stephens, P. (2020, February 13). *What I Wish Other People Understood About Losing A Child*. Mindbodygreen. https://www.mindbodygreen.com/articles/what-i-wish-other-people-understood-about-losing-a-child

Tampa Bay Compassionate Friends. (n.d.). *Grief quotes for loss of a child*. Grief Support Parents| Bereaved Grandparents | Mourning the Loss of a Child | Losing a Child | Parents Grieving. https://tampabaycompassionatefriends.org/grief-quotes-for-loss-of-a-child/

UCDavis Health. (n.d.). *Activities for Grieving Children and Families*. Health.ucdavis.edu. https://health.ucdavis.edu/children/patient-education/bereavement-activities

Vallie, S. (2022, August 25). *What to Know About Grieving the Death of a Child* (D. Paul Baby, Ed.). WebMD. https://www.webmd.com/balance/what-to-know-about-grieving-the-death-of-a-child

Vasquez, A. (2022, May 3). *What is Parental Grief and How Does It Work?* Www.joincake.com. https://www.joincake.com/blog/parents-grief/

Vasquez, A. (2023, March 28). *7 Online Grief Support Groups for Parents Who Lost a Child*. Www.joincake.com. https://www.joincake.com/blog/grief-support-groups-for-parents-who-have-lost-a-child/

Vitelli, R. (2013, February 4). *When a Parent Loses a Child* (D. Frye, Ed.). Www.psychologytoday.com. https://www.psychologytoday.com/za/blog/media-spotlight/201302/when-parent-loses-child

What's Your Grief. (2019, February 25). *64 Quotes About Grief, Coping and Life After Loss*. What's Your Grief. https://whatsyourgrief.com/64-quotes-about-grief/

Wichelns, M. (2022, October 12). *How to cope with the death of a child*. CHOC - Children's Health Hub. https://health.choc.org/how-to-cope-with-the-death-of-a-child/

Witmer, D. (2021, September). *Coping With the Sudden Death of Your Child* (A. Morin, Ed.). Verywell Family. https://www.verywellfamily.com/coping-with-the-sudden-death-of-a-child-2609745

World Health Organization. (2018). *Why We Need to Talk about Losing a Baby* (P. N. Simelela, Ed.). Www.who.int. https://www.who.int/news-room/spotlight/why-we-need-to-talk-about-losing-a-baby

Wright, M. (2012, May 7). *Two Styles of Grieving: Intuitive and Instrumental.* GoodTherapy.org Therapy Blog. https://www.goodtherapy.org/blog/styles-of-grieving-050712

Zhao, X., Hu, H., Zhou, Y., & Bai, Y. (2020). What are the long-term effects of child loss on parental health? Social integration as mediator. *Comprehensive Psychiatry, 100*(152182). https://doi.org/10.1016/j.comppsych.2020.152182

Printed in Great Britain
by Amazon